HOW TO WRITE LETTERS
FOR ALL OCCASIONS

BUSINESS LETTERS
Alexander L. Sheff

SOCIAL LETTERS
Edna Ingalls

HOW TO WRITE LETTERS
FOR ALL OCCASIONS

New Edition,
Revised by
MARY S. ALLEN

DOUBLEDAY & COMPANY, INC.
Garden City, New York

CONTENTS

Introduction to the Revised Edition

We all have to write letters, at home or at the office. Some of us may write only on occasion, others almost every day. In addition to our personal and business correspondence, from time to time we send or answer formal invitations which usually should follow certain accepted conventions in wording. The purpose of this book is to give you recommendations, suggestions, and specific models for letters appropriate to each and all of these various occasions.

Letter writing is often something that must be done, and it often seems like a chore even for fluent writers. It is our aim to help you remove some of the obstacles that can make it a chore. If letter writing is easier and pleasanter for you, your letters are likely to be better—more natural, and consequently clearer and more convincing.

At its best, writing letters is a normal and casual means of communication, a matter of readily telling someone else something that you know and he does not. Letters have to be a little more exact than conversation usually is, because in having your say in a letter your meaning has to be complete and clear. You cannot go on talking to clarify yourself. If you have thought things through, however, and your thinking is clear to you, you will probably have little trouble in transferring your thought to paper. You then may need to know only the technical formulas which you are expected to follow in putting your letter together.

This book can help you in two ways. You may want to go through it all, or parts of it, and practice writing some of the kinds of letters that apply to your needs. In this way you can develop for yourself the knack of writing letters freely, so that you will be able to keep up your correspondence with natural ease.

You can also use the book as a reference work, to look up the formalities and some terms of expression. You may need just an opening, to organize your thoughts and lead you into a letter, or you may need just a closing to get you graciously out of the letter. In this book you will find discussions of letter writing that provide specific suggestions. The many examples of letters making up the bulk of the book are models that you can follow in whole or in part. You may want to borrow some standard expressions from them, or you may be able to get from our letters inspiration for your own phrasing or for your own entire messages.

In its first edition *How to Write Letters for All Occasions* helped many people to handle their various kinds of correspondence. In revising it, we have tried to adapt it to current needs and we have modified it accordingly; but we have kept the original plan and most of the original material, both of which have proved themselves useful. The book now, as then, treats separately business letters and social letters, with a convenient breakdown of subjects under this main grouping—as shown in the Table of Contents—to help you find the models for the particular letter you need. An index at the back of the book will make it all the easier to locate specific points and pointers. We have brought the book up to date, so that the letters refer to current circumstances in a style that is now generally used. We hope you will find that they are the kind of letters you will want to write.

M. S. A.

Part One

BUSINESS LETTERS

Introduction

The first part of this book is devoted to Business Letters; the second part to Social Letters. However, the first three chapters will prove helpful to the readers of both sections, as they contain the fundamentals of all correspondence—punctuation, capitalization, and spelling—along with useful information on the tools and equipment generally used in letter writing.

The Business Letters section has been planned for men and women now in business and for those who expect to enter this field. It is for both employers and employees—for manufacturers, shopkeepers, office managers, and secretaries—and it is also for customers, for anyone who may need to write to business concerns.

Chapter by chapter, this book takes up nearly every kind of business correspondence. In addition to detailed instructions, each chapter presents many sample letters to use as guides in the writing of that particular type of letter. The subjects covered include routine letters of acknowledgment, inquiry, and confirmation; letters about goods and services; letters of complaint and adjustment; letters about credit and collection; sales letters; personal business letters; letters of application for positions, and replies to them.

Just as your speech and dress express your personality, so your letters represent you on paper. In showing you how to master correct form and clarity of expression, this book will help you to create a good impression in your letters, as well as obtain the specific results you want. You will find that more effective business letters mean greater business success.

A. L. S.

Chapter One

MAKING YOUR
LETTER ATTRACTIVE

Your business letter represents your firm just as the personality of its salesmen and the quality of its goods or services do. Therefore, you want your letters to make the best possible impression on those who receive them.

Start out with a typewriter that is in good condition and has the appropriate size of type. Be sure that the ribbon is clean so that it does not smudge or print too faintly. Use a good quality letter paper that suits the type of business you are engaged in. Make your letterhead reflect the personality of your firm, and finally, see that your envelopes match your stationery.

SELECTING THE RIGHT TOOLS

Your Paper

Most business firms use 8½ x 11 inch letter size paper. This is found to be the most convenient for general correspondence. Other firms, however, use letter paper that is 7¼ x 10½ inches, and a few firms use half-sheets for general correspondence, but this 5½ x 8½ inch size is more commonly used for memoranda on which only a few lines are written.

The quality of the paper should be as fine as the firm can afford. White paper is more commonly used than tinted, but businesses that wish to obtain a special effect frequently use a lightly colored paper.

Your Letterhead

Modern business letterheads are dignified and simple, in contrast to the old-fashioned letterheads that usually were very ornate, with an excess of printed matter. The name and address of the firm, institution, or individual, should be placed at the top of the letterhead. The same face of type in various sizes is always good form on letterheads and envelopes. Any good printer will design and print the right kind of letterhead and envelope that will be in keeping with your business requirements.

Your Envelopes

As a general rule, envelopes should match the letterhead in color, quality, and weight. A variety of sizes are available but the most frequently used are the commercial (6¼ or 6¾ size), the large official (No. 9 or No. 10), and the legal size.

Your Typewriter

With very few exceptions, all modern business letters are written on a typewriter. The two sizes of type most generally used are *pica* and *élite*.

Pica is by far the more common and practical size of type for the average business. It is larger than élite and, because of its size, makes clearer carbon copies. However, many businesses and professions prefer élite type because of its dignified appearance. Few business houses use both sizes of type.

Black typewriter ribbons are the most commonly used for business letters. However, if you write on tinted paper or stationery with colored headings, you may want to use a typewriter ribbon to harmonize with it.

Since you would not send out damaged merchandise, you must not mail any damaged letters. Letters should be free from smudges, erasures, and blots. Words crossed out and rewritten and words added between the lines make an equally poor impression.

Your business letters should always be *neat, readable, dignified, businesslike*.

When you have mastered the following details, you can devote your attention to the content of your letters.

HOW TO USE YOUR TOOLS

When you have selected the right tools, you will want to use them with the greatest of care. You could own the finest clothes yet not be well-dressed unless you kept your clothes in order and wore them at the right times. Attractiveness in letter writing is largely a matter of spacing your lines, watching your margins, neatly organizing the various elements in your letters, and folding the letters for convenient opening.

Spacing the Typewriter Lines

Most long letters are single-spaced, with double spaces between paragraphs. Short letters may be double-spaced, with triple spaces between paragraphs. However, when the paragraphs are indented, as is more common, double spacing between them is correct.

In a single-spaced letter, four spaces should be left between the date and the address of the recipient. Two spaces should be left between the address and the salutation ("Dear Sir" or "Dear Madam"), between the salutation and the beginning of the body of the letter, between the end of the body of the letter and the complimentary close. Four spaces are usually left between the complimentary close and the typed name of the sender, but this space may be varied according to the size of the handwriting.

Width of Margins

Letters are bound by margins at the top and bottom, and on both sides. The width of these margins is an important factor toward the attractive appearance of all letters.

The width of the margin varies with the length of the letter. Long letters have narrow margins (top and bottom, and at the sides).

When the letter is long, the margin on the left side should be at least an inch wide, and the margin on the right should be approximately the same.

Top and bottom margins should be about equal in depth. Most letters have engraved or printed headings. When the letter covers a full page, the margin should begin from one to one-and-a-half

inches below the base of the letterhead. And when there is no
engraved or printed heading, or when the letter runs over to a
second page, the top margin should be about one-and-a-half
inches. When the letter is shorter, the top margin can be deeper
with the bottom margin correspondingly higher. The second page
of a letter should have the same width of margin as the first, and
the last page should, of course, have the same margins at the
top and sides, but end wherever convenient.

The second page of a letter is just as important as the first, and
the paper should be of the same size, quality, and color. It should
be headed at the *left* with the name of the correspondent; in the
center with the number of the page; and at the *right* with the
date. In the event that the pages of the letter get separated, this
data will help you or your correspondent to identify them.

Under no circumstances should an ordinary business letter be
continued on the *back* of a sheet. Never write a business letter
on both sides of a page.

Folding the Letter

Letter paper should always be a trifle narrower than the length
of the envelope so that the letter will fit into it easily. The number
of folds depends on the size of the envelope. The No. 10 envelope is the size most commonly used and requires that letter
paper be folded the long way into three equal parts. For short
envelopes, an 8½-by-11 sheet is folded first in half, then triple
on the side.

In folding a page the edges should not be brought exactly
even. The letter will be somewhat easier to unfold if one end
extends slightly beyond the other. It must extend only a small
fraction of an inch to remain neat, however, and the depth of
the fold must be equal, the sides of the page remaining even.

Chapter Two

THE PARTS OF
THE LETTER

The arrangement of the different parts of a business letter makes a world of difference in the impression it conveys. It is no more suitable for a letter to go out without the proper date line, salutation and other elements, than it would be for the head of a large concern to call on a client in slacks and tennis shoes. Unless a business letter follows the accepted correct form, the person receiving it may very well discredit the company that has sent it out.

The business world expects certain formalities in letters from reputable firms, and woe to the letter writer who neglects them. For the most part, these formalities are simply a matter of neatness.

Specifically, a business letter involves six parts:

1. heading
2. inside address
3. salutation
4. body of the letter
5. complimentary close
6. signature

Sometimes there is a seventh part, the postscript.

THE HEADING

The heading, in full, consists of the address of the sender and the letter's date. However, most business paper is engraved or printed with a letterhead giving the name of the company, as well as its address. (Properly speaking, the *letterhead* is the printed matter itself, not the sheet of paper, as it sometimes is thought to be.) When the address is printed, the heading to be typed need consist of only the date.

Here is an example:

ROBERT C. JONES ELECTRONICS CO.

444 Beal Street

Cleveland 14, Ohio

January 12, 19—

A printed heading is usually centered at the top of the sheet. When you write on paper without a letterhead, the typed heading may include the firm's name, but not an individual person's name. No matter what it contains, it is written toward the upper right side of the paper.

Headings may be written in either "step" or "block" form. In the step heading, each line after the first is indented beyond the preceding one.

3 Astor Place

New York, N. Y.

June 27, 19—

In the block heading, which is more common nowadays, all the lines are written flush with the first one.

378 Lexington Avenue

New York, N. Y.

July 8, 19—

Occasionally social secretaries and professional studios use an unusual type of heading, such as:

June

23

19—

To avoid the possibility of any misunderstanding on the part of the person to whom you are writing, it is very important that you make the date of your letter perfectly clear. The name of the month should be spelled out in full. An abbreviation may or may not be clear enough, but it is too informal for almost any business letter. It usually is not adequate to write only numerals (such as 10/7/61) for the date. In the first place, it gives an impression of hurriedness, and in the second place, it is easily misunderstood. Americans would read the date "October 7, 1961," but most Europeans, including the British, read it "July 10, 1961," as Europeans read the numbers as day, month, and year, and Americans read them as month, day, and year.

The beginning of the date, at the top of the page, and the beginning of the complimentary close, at the bottom of the page, should line up.

THE INSIDE ADDRESS

The beginning of the inside address contains the name and address of the firm or individual to whom you are writing. This is important primarily because it makes a record on the carbon copy, enabling you to identify the letter for filing purposes.

The inside address should be in line with the left-hand margin. It should start two to four lines below the last line of the heading. Either the step or block form may be used. The block form is much quicker, because no time is lost in indenting each line.

In general, there are three kinds of addresses.

(1) To an individual in a firm:

> Mr. John J. Wiley
> Ajax Oil Company
> 246 Broadway
> Oklahoma City 5, Okla.

(2) To an anonymous official in the firm:

> The Traffic Manager
> Benton Bolt Company
> 344 Rue Road
> Chicago 39, Ill.

(3) To the firm itself:

> Peter J. Rowe Hat Co.
> 33 Lafayette Street
> Tampico, Fla.

Sometimes another kind of address is used. A letter can be directed to the attention of a department head, although anyone in the firm may open it:

> Junior Miss Style Co.
> 444 Seventh Avenue
> New York 16, N. Y.

> Attention of the Advertising Manager

or:

> Attention: Advertising Manager

If you wish to address your letter to the attention of a particular person, follow the form just given, but change the extra line to read:

> Attention of Mr. John K. Jones

"Attention of" is usually indented, and two spaces usually are left between the address and this line, as well as between this line and the salutation. The "Attention" line may or may not be underscored, and it is sometimes abbreviated, "Att."

In social and form letters, the inside address may be written at the foot of the letter and to the left of the signature. The margin in this case is the same as it would be if the address were placed at the top.

The examples we have used are in an "unpunctuated" or "open" style; that is, they have only the normal punctuation of general usage. If you prefer to use a "punctuated" or "closed" style for the inside address, place a comma after each line except the last, which requires a period. This style is rare now. Of course, a period should always be placed after abbreviations and initials.

The titles "Mr.," "Miss," "Mrs." or a substitute form should never be omitted from the inside address. However, never use "Mr." with a name when you are writing "Esq." (Esquire) after it. The proper form is, *John Hammond Smith, Esq.*

When writing to a woman, always address her as she signs herself. It is considered correct to address a woman as "Miss," unless she has signed herself as "Mrs."

"Messrs." is used in addressing partners, as:

Messrs. Smythe & Weston

While American professors and holders of other than medical degrees do not use their titles as frequently as Europeans, these titles, as well as others, should be used in a business letter. For instance:

Dr. Charles Brown
Charles Brown, M.D.
Prof. James Smith
Rev. Harold Jones
Hon. John Black

("Hon." is used for senators, congressmen, ambassadors, governors, judges, mayors, and heads of government departments.)

For greater formality, Prof., Rev. and Hon. should be spelled out, as follows: Professor, The Reverend, The Honorable.

Other forms of address used for government officials and church dignitaries are listed on pages 137 and 156 respectively.

THE SALUTATION

The salutation in a business letter is simply the formal written equivalent of "Hello" or "Good Morning." It should be written flush with the first line and two spaces below the last line of the inside address. The only punctuation needed after the salutation is the colon (:). Salutations most commonly used are:

Dear Madam:
Dear Sir:
My dear Madam:

My dear Sir:
Gentlemen:
Dear Sirs:
Dear Mr. Bronson:
My dear Mrs. Green:

Note that in the more formal "My dear Sir," the word "dear" is not capitalized. A woman, whether married or not, is addressed as "Dear Madam." If the writer is acquainted with the correspondent—or if the writer's business has to do with the correspondent himself, directly—the less formal "Dear Mr. Jones," should be used. If you are writing informally to a personal business friend, address the person as "Dear Bill" or "Dear Sally."

When writing to a firm, the expression "Gentlemen" is more common than "Dear Sirs," though the latter is in perfectly good taste. Only in letters to government officials, should you use formal salutations "Sir" or "Sirs" (without the word "Dear"). When writing to a firm where employer and associates are women, the salutation should be "Mesdames."

Form letters, or circular letters, can be addressed directly either to groups of people or to individuals. Common examples are:

Dear Readers:
Dear Newsdealer:
Dear Co-workers:
Dear Customer:

Because such salutations are a little cold, many firms prefer using a personal heading inserted into the form letters to read specifically, "Dear Mrs. Smith," and so forth, taking the name from the mailing list.

THE BODY OF THE LETTER

The body of the letter is the main part of the message, the subject matter. Here is an example of a typical business letter, complete with Heading, Inside Address, Salutation, and Body.

34 Main Street,
Johnstown, Illinois,
August 3, 19——.

Mr. Roger G. Baldwin,
740 Dakota Street,
Billville, South Dakota.

Dear Sir:

Thank you for your letter of July 28.

We are sorry that there has been a slight delay in filling your order. As you may know, we are now working on a full 24-hour schedule, and we have found it difficult to obtain sufficient raw materials. You will be pleased, however, to know that we can definitely ship your order by next Thursday at the latest.

We hope we have not inconvenienced you.

The body of the letter may consist of only one paragraph, or of as many paragraphs as you need to convey your message clearly and pleasantly. Paragraphs may be either in block or indented form. When using the block form, the first line of each paragraph begins flush with your left-hand margin. And when using the other form, indent from five to ten spaces at the beginning of each paragraph. Indented style for paragraphs is more common.

It is advisable that even in a comparatively short letter separate paragraphs should be made of the beginning, the body of the letter, and the closing paragraph. This makes your message appear neater and easier to read and understand. If each paragraph contains only one major statement, the total structure and purpose of your letter can be grasped most easily.

THE COMPLIMENTARY CLOSE

Just as the salutation is a letter's equivalent of "Good Morning," so the complimentary close is an equivalent for "Good-by." "Yours truly" is one of the forms most commonly used, but there are many from which to choose:

Yours very truly,
Very truly yours,
Yours respectfully,
Yours very respectfully,
Very respectfully yours,
Sincerely yours,

Yours sincerely,
Sincerely,
Faithfully yours,
Very faithfully yours,
Yours faithfully,
Cordially yours,
Very cordially yours,
Yours cordially,

The correct complimentary close is the one most appropriate for your purpose. Each implies a different degree of formality or friendship. The complimentary close should mean what it says. You would hardly write "Yours cordially" to someone you were about to sue, or "Yours respectfully" to a personal acquaintance.

THE SIGNATURE

The signature, the name of the person who wrote or dictated the letter, should always be written by hand. A rubber stamp makes a poor showing. The signature should be written legibly. Usually, the signature is typed first, and the name of the sender is written above the typed signature, to avoid all possibilities of misunderstanding, without losing the necessary personal touch.

The name of the writer is all the signature required in a letter coming from an individual.

Yours truly,
Alfred Johnson

When the writer represents a firm, and its name is not printed in the letterhead, the name should be typed to follow the signature. There are several ways of doing this:

Yours truly,

Alfred Johnson, Office Manager
South Philadelphia Hat Company

Yours truly,

THE MASON & JONES COMPANY
By_____

Between the complimentary close and the typed signature, four spaces are usually allowed. The number of spaces left for the written signature depends on the size of the handwriting. If the firm name is used after the complimentary close, sufficient space must still be left for the handwritten signature.

If a letter is dictated, the stenographer gives in the lower left-hand corner the initials of the person who dictated it and her own initials, so that the letter can be easily identified. This is usually done as follows: JP/AJ, TF:HH (or JP/aj, TF:hh), indicating that John Palmer dictated to Anne Jackson, Thomas Foster to Harriet Howe, for example.

A secretary may have to sign her employer's name—the letter may have to go out quickly when he is not available—in which case she may write his name, if so instructed, with her own initials below the signature. She may be asked to sign her own full name and write "for" with her employer's name.

When something is enclosed with a letter—a pamphlet, bill, notice, check, a copy of another letter, etc.—attention should be called to it by writing "Enclosure" or "Enc." or "Enclosures." Type this under sender's and stenographer's initials. Beneath the word "Enclosure," the item or items may be mentioned specifically:

Enclosures:
  Annual Catalog of Publications
  Dictionary of Garden Terms

Sometimes, a carbon copy of a letter is sent to someone mentioned in it. His name should be written in the lower left, so that it will appear on both copies:

Copy to:
  Mr. Alfred Jones

or:

  cc: Mr. Alfred Jones

THE OUTSIDE ADDRESS

The outside address, which goes on the envelope, follows the form of the inside address, either block or step, and should be typed on the envelope a little toward the right center. However, when the names making up the address are long, the writing should start nearer the left center of the envelope to give a well-balanced appearance.

A line beginning with "Attention of," or "Personal," should be typed at the lower left-hand side.

If a letter is being sent by Air Mail and/or Special Delivery, these words should be typed at the upper right-hand side, immediately under the postage stamp or stamps, or to the left of center below the level of the address.

Chapter Three

THE LANGUAGE
OF THE LETTER

Three basic tools for writing any letters are punctuation, spelling, and grammar. This chapter is devoted to the more important rules of punctuation and capitalization, as well as to the more common errors in English and the ways of avoiding them.

A GUIDE TO PUNCTUATION

It is impossible to put too much emphasis on the importance of correct punctuation. Its purpose is to break your sentences up into easily read parts, in order to make your meaning clear. It plays the same role in writing that pauses and emphasis do in speaking.

Incorrect punctuation can change the entire meaning of a sentence. Leaving out periods, commas or other punctuation marks, or putting them in the wrong places, can result in your writing something contrary to what you intended to say.

The Period (.)

The period should be used at the end of every statement. It should be used at the end of every request. "We have your letter." "Please send 5 gross of pins." There are only three punctuation marks with which to end sentences: the period, the question mark, and the exclamation point.

The period should also be used to indicate that you have used an abbreviation, as in: "Mr." which stands for "Mister," "Dr." for "Doctor," "Oct." for "October," etc.

The Comma (,)

The comma indicates a short break in a sentence, and is used to make the meaning clear and the reading easy. A long sentence can be unintelligible without the proper use of commas. Notice the difference between the following sentences:

The goods you sent us which we ordered last May would have been fine items to sell our customers the cannery workers if they had not come after the peak season ending in June.

This sentence may need a rereading, but when properly punctuated, it is easily understood:

The goods you sent us, which we ordered last May, would have been fine items to sell our customers, the cannery workers, if they had not come after the peak season, ending in June.

In general, the comma should be used in the same way that you would use a pause in speaking, to break up a sentence into its parts of varying importance.

The basic rules for the use of the comma are:

(1) The comma is used to set off phrases and words that have a parenthetic function, usually adding emphasis rather than facts, as the following: *that is, in fact, of course, it so happens that,* etc.

(2) To set off words in apposition; that is, terms identifying previous terms:

Mr. Jones, our salesman, will call on you.

(3) To separate a quotation from the rest of the sentence:

Mr. Green said, "Please call on us."
"Not this week," your representative told us.

(4) To show that a word grammatically necessary is left out:

To err is human; to forgive, divine.

(5) To separate clauses which are joined by one of the co-ordinate conjunctions: *and, but, for, either, or, neither, nor;* or by subordinate conjunctions: *who, that, which, because, since, as, while,* etc.; in subordinate clauses that stand apart, further describing ("nonrestrictive"), rather than identifying ("restrictive"), an object:

The goods that you ordered are not in stock, but the shipment, which we will send by air express, will be made when we get them.

(6) To separate lists of words:

We ran short of cigarettes, candy, soda, pie, etc.

(7) To divide a sentence where identical or similar words follow one another in a way that otherwise would be confusing:

If you do it, do it now.

(8) To set off the name of the person you are addressing:

Mr. James, please send us the coffee data.

(9) To divide series of figures into thousands, millions, etc.:

7,585   57,585   8,564,784   585,758,494

(10) After the complimentary close of a letter:

Yours truly,

John Arnold

(11) To separate the parts of an address when written in "closed" style or in straight paragraph form:

Southern Home Baked Pie Corp., 239 Fall River Road, Hampton, Virginia.

(12) To separate the day of the month from the year, the day of the week from the month:

Thursday, September 3, 19——.

The Semicolon (;)

A semicolon indicates a shorter pause than a period, but a longer pause than a comma. It is used if a long sentence could well be broken into shorter ones but the thought is held together better when the break is not so sharp. It also serves to separate a series of clauses or phrases that already contain commas.

This is what we can do for you: we can send part of your order now, that is, the Beethoven and Brahms records; we can send the whole order later on; or we can cancel the order, letting you take a chance on filling it elsewhere immediately.

The Colon (:)

The colon is used:

As an introduction to something that follows.

In salutations to letters, as, "Dear Sir:" (No dash or hyphen is required after the colon. "Dear Sir:—" is wrong.)

After expressions such as: "for example:", "to wit:", "for instance:", "the following:".

The Question Mark (?)

The question mark should be used after a direct question.

When can we expect shipment?

An indirect question (which is put as a subordinate clause) does *not* need a question mark.

We want to know when we can expect shipment.

When two or more questions follow each other, a question mark should be used after each. A question mark may come within a sentence, if the sentence extends beyond the direct question itself:

Will you call on us? or shall we call on you?
Are our customers content? is our first concern.

The Exclamation Point (!)

The exclamation point indicates an emphatic statement that denotes surprise, emotion or doubt.

The customer paid cash!
We just can not put up with it!
He says he shipped it!

The exclamation point is used after exclamations which seldom occur in business letters, such as: oh! ah! alas! ouch!

Unless it is used rarely, only when there is real cause for excitement, the exclamation point defeats its own purpose. Most sentences carry more emphasis without exclamation points than they would with them. Too many writers use exclamation points to lend excitement to sentences that are really not exciting at all.

The Dash (—)

The dash is used in a sentence where the thought is suddenly interrupted. It often serves the purpose of colon, semicolon, or comma, but it is usually better to use one of them than a dash if you have a clear case for doing so. The dash should be saved for special emphasis or for a time when the structure of your sentence cannot be as clear without it:

Every time we ask you for your payment, now five months overdue —and that we sincerely regret to say, has had to be very often—you put us off with an excuse.

A comma should not be used before the dash, as "often,—you." Use the dash alone, as "often—you." In typing, a space is usually left before and after a dash. The dash is typed as two hyphens together.

The Hyphen (-)

The hyphen is used to connect parts of words. It is also used when a word has to be divided between syllables at the end of a line:

> Split-level
> Air-conditioned
> Editor-in-chief

> Unfortunately, we are un-
> able to deliver your order.
> It is useless to wait indefi-
> nitely for his reply.

Be sure to divide such words by syllables, just as they are divided in the dictionary. See "Syllabication" below.

Parentheses ( )

Parentheses make a slightly stronger break in a sentence than commas or dashes. They are most often used to enclose statements or references which amplify or explain the thought of the sentence. For example:

The fine brushes you sent us (and when I say "fine," I really mean it) are selling like hot cakes.

Parentheses are also used to enclose the figures of an amount that has been spelled out, such as: two hundred dollars ($200), etc.

Figures may be put in parentheses when a list is numbered consecutively: (1), (2), (3).

The Apostrophe (')

The apostrophe is used in forming possessives, and to indicate the omission of one or more letters in a word.

In most cases, the adding of the apostrophe and *s* forms the possessive, as in: *John's hat, the company's headquarters, the month's billing.*

In plural nouns, the apostrophe usually comes after the *s*, as in: *the two companies' headquarters, the three months' billings.*

Where the plural is not formed by *s*, the apostrophe is used in the same way it is in singular nouns, as for example: *women's clothing, men's hats, children's habits.*

When words that are singular end in *s*, only the apostrophe usually is placed after the word, as in: *Mathematics' laws are irrefutable.* Sometimes, however, another *s* is added: *Success's first sign.*

Examples of contractions, words from which one or more letters have been omitted are:

Can't—*for* cannot
Don't—*for* do not
I'm—*for* I am
He's—*for* he is

Quotation Marks (" ")

Quotation marks are used to enclose quotations which represent the exact words originally spoken or written.

The client said: "Sold!"

When a quotation is presented within a quotation, single quotation marks are used.

He said: "When you answered, 'yes,' I wired the home office right away."

When the quotation takes up several paragraphs, quotation marks are placed at the beginning of each paragraph, but at the end of only the last paragraph.

CAPITALIZATION

Capitals should be used as follows:

(1) To begin the first word of every sentence.
(2) For proper names in general, names of people, business

firms, organizations, government committees, government boards, political parties, names of holidays, cities and states, months of the year, and days of the week.

(3) For the words, *North, South, East,* and *West* and their compounds, *Northwest, Southeast,* etc., when they indicate parts of the country or of the world, rather than merely a direction.

(4) For the title of an individual when it accompanies the name.

(5) For the first word of a quotation, as in:

He said, "They will come."

SPELLING

If you don't know how to spell a word, look it up in the dictionary. Most accurate spellers avoid mistakes because they have learned to spell each word individually rather than because they have mastered a set of spelling rules.

The most frequent spelling mistakes are those to be found in the *ie* and *ei* words. When they occur together, the letter *i* almost always comes first, unless a *c* comes before the combination.

Common exceptions to this rule are: *either, height, foreign, seize, neighbor, financier, weird, leisure, neither.* Some tricky words which do follow the rule are:

ie	*ei*
believe	ceiling
relief	conceive
relieve	deceit
siege	perceive
sieve	receive

SYLLABICATION

Syllabication is the separation of words into syllables. This is not only a guide to pronunciation, but a guide to the correct division of a word when there is not room at the end of a line to write the entire word.

If you are at all doubtful about dividing a word into syllables, be sure to look it up in your dictionary. You will find, for example, that the word finger is written *fin'ger*. Should you have to split this word at the end of a line, you would write *fin-* at the end of the line and *ger* at the beginning of the next.

Words of one syllable are not supposed to be divided, even though they are rather long, such as: *width, waived, passed, mailed, filed, bounced,* etc.

WRITING HINTS

It is true that the mechanics of the business letter, and the rules of punctuation, spelling and the like, are far simpler than the actual job of writing. But many people stare for minutes at a blank piece of paper, wondering how to begin, just because they have allowed themselves to build up a set of mental hazards. As a matter of fact, a little practice should convince anyone that it is as easy to write as it is to talk. If you can make a request or place an order orally, you can quickly learn to do so on paper.

The first thing to do in writing a business letter is to make sure of your facts. Then decide on the order of importance of the things you wish to say, and your letter is half written. It is really as easy as that.

Let us suppose that you wish to order a shipment of shoes. When you have before you the name and address of the concern to which you are writing, when you know the sizes, quantity, price and desired date of shipment of the shoes, you can hardly fail to write a good business letter.

Your letter, for instance, might read something like this:

Dear Sir:
    Please ship the following not later than May 3:
        3 dozen Women's Oxfords, assorted sizes, at $8.00 a pair.
    Our check for $288.00 in payment of this order is enclosed.

                              Yours truly,

This is a very simple form of business letter. But it is typical of all good business letters inasmuch as it is brief and to the point. Just as brevity is the soul of wit, so is brevity the soul of a business letter. Unlike the old-fashioned business letter which made use of many ornate, formal phrases, the modern business letter is as streamlined as a racing car. But under no circumstances should courtesy and clearness be sacrificed for brevity. The shortest business letter should always take time to be polite. And it must be as frank and open as a business conversation so that your correspondent will be convinced of your sincerity.

Many business letters do not have to go out of their way to be interesting. This is true of letters that place orders, answer inquiries, arrange for meetings and the like. But the letter which is written to persuade someone to do something is another story. This may be a sales letter; a letter asking for employment, for credit, and so on. You may have to interest the reader sufficiently for him to want to comply with your wishes. An example illustrating this type of letter follows:

Dear Sir:

As you know, we have done very well with the last shipment of fountain pens which you sent us. We sold the whole lot in a little less than two weeks. And we expect to do even better in the future.

You can help us to do this, if you will. We have outstanding a number of bills which we expect will be paid to us within two weeks. Until then, we can order only the regular shipment of fountain pens on a cash basis. But if you are willing to extend our credit until the end of the month, we can place an order for double that amount with you.

Please let us know by Monday whether or not you can accommodate us.

Yours sincerely,

Notice that this letter talks about the correspondent's interests right from the start, and gives him an opportunity to make bigger sales. The language is simple and clear. In other letters, a richer style may be desirable. In all such letters there is one essential— a promise that the reader will get something from you, such as bigger sales, if he extends credit; a bargain, if he buys your product; a more effective organization, if he gives you the job for which you are applying.

Many people think that there is a special language called "Business English" which is supposed to be somewhat different from everyday spoken English. Frequently this concept complicates the job of writing to a person with whom you are doing business. But the average business letter is written, not in some special "Business English," but in the familiar language which you use all day.

A business letter is usually shorter and more specific than a social letter. It may employ expressions used only in business, such as "order," "remit," "liabilities," "overhead." These expressions are used just as engineers, doctors, and chemists use specialized terms in their dealings with each other.

There was a time when business letters were stiff and formal, but today the tendency is to write in a simple, natural, almost conversational way. Business correspondence ranges from letters that are almost as brief as telegrams, to more lengthy and intimate letters, depending on how well you know the person with whom you are dealing, and the requirements of your subject matter.

The best way to write a business letter is to make it conform as closely as possible to spoken English. Let us suppose that you have just received a letter from a wholesaler. He has promised you a shipment of goods which is late in arriving. You might telephone him and say:

"Mr. Jones? How are you? This is Bill Rogers, of Rogers and Pratt. We've just received your letter about the shipment of brass couplings, but there seems to be some delay. I'm afraid our work is being held up until we get them. Would you be able to look into this and see that we get the couplings as soon as possible? Thank you. I know you'll do your best for us. Good-by."

If you decided to write to Mr. Jones instead of telephoning him, your letter might read:

Dear Mr. Jones:

Thank you for your letter of March 12, in which you promised immediate shipment of the brass couplings we ordered on March 6.

This shipment is several days overdue, and our work is being held up.

Could you please look into this and see what you can do about getting these couplings to us as soon as possible.

We know you will do your best.

Yours cordially,

As you see, this typical business letter closely follows the telephone call. It is clear, brief, and polite.

Avoiding "Dead" Expressions

Business letters used to be studded with stiff phrases, which, it seems, were intended to give business a sort of dignity. But now that business has come into its own, these expressions are simply old-fashioned. We can be perfectly courteous without them, and we can be a great deal clearer and simpler, too. In fact, such expressions sound either affected or clumsy.

Don't say: We beg to acknowledge your esteemed favor on September 16.
Say: We have received your letter of September 16.

Don't say: Your letter at hand.
Say: We have your letter.

Don't say: We shall advise you.
Say: We shall let you know.

Don't say: As per your letter.
Say: According to your letter; *or,* As your letter says.

Don't say: And oblige.
Say: Thank you; *or,* thank you very much.

Don't say: We have your order and will forward same. (Your correspondent knows that you have his order; otherwise you wouldn't be writing about it.)
Say: We will forward your order at once.

Don't say: Thank you for yours of the 10th inst.
Say: Thank you for your letter of May 10.

Other expressions to be avoided are:

Don't say	*Say*
Enclosed please find	We enclose
We take pleasure	We are glad
Hand you a check	Send you a check
Owing to the fact that	Because
As to your proposition	Regarding your proposition
At an early date	Soon
At the present writing	Now
Even date	Today
In re the matter of	Regarding

Chapter Four

ROUTINE BUSINESS LETTERS

It should be the aim of every business office to answer all its mail the same day it is received. If for any good reason this is not possible, acknowledgment of the receipt of all letters should be made by the following day or so. (See *Stopgap Letters* below.)

That all letters should be clear and courteous, goes without saying.

Here are model letters, sentences, and phrases that may be used as a guide for the writing of the various types of business letters considered "routine" in most offices.

ACKNOWLEDGMENTS

Mr. Howard Manchester
37 Jones Street
Little Falls, Minnesota

Dear Mr. Manchester:

We have your letter of June 10, and we are very pleased to hear from you.

You may be assured that we will take up the matter you discussed with our Board of Directors as soon as possible. We shall be able to give you an answer within a week.

Yours sincerely,

Mrs. John H. Hoyt
27 Jane Street
Denver 3, Colorado

Dear Madam:

We were pleased to receive your inquiry. We carry a full line of straw hats, as the enclosed catalogue shows. Our price list is attached.

Your order will be greatly appreciated.

Very truly yours,

Mr. James Pearson
110 High Street
Minneapolis 12, Minnesota

Dear Mr. Pearson:

Thank you for your letter of December 3. Because we have done business with each other for so long, I am going to make you a rather unusual proposition.

Present available prices are perfectly reasonable, but if you are buying for your spring trade we think you will do better to wait until the first of the year.

If anything changes in the meantime I shall be very glad to let you know.

Cordially yours,

Beaver, Beaver & Smith
211 MacDougal Street
Boston 21, Mass.

Gentlemen:

Thank you for your request for samples and price quotations on Majestic Metal Clips.

Please allow us a few days to determine a price that would be fair for both of us for the quantity you need. You may expect to hear from us late this week.

Very truly yours,

Mr. Harold Jasper
1900 Avenue C
New York 5, N. Y.

Dear Mr. Jasper:

Ordinarily we would give an immediate answer to your inquiry. However, we are in the middle of considering a change of policy. We shall be able to advise you by July 7th.

Yours sincerely,

Bates and Brown
Denver, Ohio

Dear Sirs:

We note that you have sent us your check for $15.17, whereas your total debt comes to $18.03. We have made a thorough check of our books and think that the error is yours.

Please look into this as soon as you can, and if you agree you owe us the remainder, please send it sometime this week because we are eager to clear up our books for you.

Yours truly,

Acme Garment Co.
Barretsville, Mich.

Gentlemen:

Thank you for your letter of July 12. We have just placed an order for our summer sportswear, but we'd certainly like to keep you in mind for the Florida season.

Why don't you have your salesman drop in to see us as soon as he visits this area?

Very truly yours,

Mr. W. W. Dawson, Pres.
Dawson-Jones Corp.
347 Fifth Street,
Boone, Conn.

Dear Mr. Dawson:

Thank you for your order of December 2.

We are prepared to ship immediately 36 pairs of white suede

gloves, if you think that you can use the B Models instead of the C. Since most of our customers have found these satisfactory, we feel that you will too.

There is only a very slight difference in quality, but the low price makes these a very popular item.

Please let us know by phone or telegram by tomorrow evening.

Sincerely yours,

Opening Sentences and Phrases

This is to acknowledge your letter of April 1. We are shipping immediately 4 dozen pepper mills—812-B—F.O.B. Manchester, Vermont. You should receive them within 2 or 3 days.

This is to confirm your wire dated May 14. We agree wholeheartedly with everything you say and will sign the contract as soon as you come into our office.

Regarding your telegram of July 7, we find it impossible to accept the conditions you set down.

Thank you for your letter dated August 12.

We were pleased to receive your letter of September 3.

The letter you mentioned in our telephone conversation has just reached us.

Thank you for such a quick confirmation of our telephone agreement.

The letter you referred to in last night's conversation has not yet reached us.

In reply to your letter of May 6, we are sorry to say that——.

We are sorry but the garment you described in your letter of July 8 cannot be repaired.

It is with great regret that we have to tell you we cannot fill your order of November 11.

You will be glad to know that the request you made in your letter of July 27 has already been passed on to our vice-president.

In answer to your letter of May 3.

Your letter of May 17 asks us to send you three bales of——.

Referring further to your inquiry of September 11.

Thank you for your letter, dated December 14. I will write about it immediately to our field manager.

Your telegram has just arrived. The order will be shipped tomorrow morning.

Thank you for your check.

We were pleased to receive your check in this morning's mail.

We are glad to learn from your letter of December 17 that——.

Ending Sentences and Phrases

We hope to hear from you soon.

Will you please tell us without delay what your wishes are in this matter?

Please tell us your decision by return mail.

We are holding the goods while awaiting your reply.

We are always pleased to be of service to you in any way.

Please ask us for any further prices and samples you might want to have.

Please call on us when you need any further typewriter repairs.

STOPGAP LETTERS

Sometimes letters cannot be answered right away. In that case they should be acknowledged promptly, with an explanation for the delay. This often happens when information has been asked for and cannot be immediately answered or when the person to whom the letter is addressed is away from the office. Here are fragments of suitable letters:

This is to acknowledge the samples which you sent to Mr. Foreman. Unfortunately, he has been called away from the office for a week. He will get in touch with you the moment he gets back.

Thank you for your inquiry of May 12. Unfortunately, we do not have all the information at our fingertips. A good deal will have to come from our branch office in Hartford. As soon as we get it, we will send all the details to you. Please be patient for a few days until we are able to write you again.

Thank you for your order of July 7. We are not yet sure whether or not we will be able to send you as many as two dozen gas generating machines. We could send you one dozen now and hold up your order for the others. Please let us know what you want to do.

The subject you are interested in will be brought up at the next meeting of the board of directors.

We are investigating the matter and will report to you as soon as we have the information.

LETTERS OF CONFIRMATION

Mr. Hugo Bromfield
712 Elm Street
Ridgewood, New Jersey

Dear Mr. Bromfield:
This is in reference to the call which your Mr. James made at our office this morning.
We hereby confirm the arrangements made between us about your terms and discount. In order to keep the record straight, here are the full terms of the agreement:

(Text of Agreement)

If this is all right please confirm the arrangements; otherwise, please point out any inaccuracies so that they can be corrected right away.

Very truly yours,

Sentences and Phrases

It was nice to have a phone talk with you this morning. We are sending you samples immediately and will give you the price of 14¢ a pair.

Thank you for your call today. I look forward with pleasure to seeing you tomorrow (Tuesday) at 10:30.

I will be delighted to see you at 11:00 tomorrow morning. Please bring a contract with you. It will be a pleasure to sign it.

This is to confirm our telephone conversation today. Our Mr. Abernathy will be delighted to see you at 10:30 tomorrow morning. Please bring samples of your work with you.

Confirming the agreement we came to last Thursday, we shall undertake to——.

With further reference to the matter we discussed yesterday——.

MAKING INQUIRIES AND REQUESTS

In requesting information or some service either for yourself or for a business, clarity and courtesy are of obvious importance. You are asking somebody to do something for you, so you want to show that you will be appreciative of his help. You can be as pleasant to deal with through your letter as you would try to be in person. If you are writing for a business, of course, your letter, as always, represents the firm's reputation. Through inquiries to other firms, as well as in the services of your own, business relationships are smoothed and developed.

You will make yourself easy to be helped most of all by being as clear and specific as you can. Ask for just what you want with an unmistakable description of your need. You will want to be particularly certain that your return address is easy to read.

Mr. William R. Brown
Wilton, N. Y.

Dear Bill:

This may be a trade secret. But what are a few secrets between old friends? I am very eager to know who designed the packages you are using for your prunes. That is one of the most striking packages I have seen this season, and I would certainly like to see your designer doing some work for me. Since we are not competitors (at least in business), I hope you will be glad to send us this information with the speed of light.

Sincerely,

Jones-Smith Corporation
Potter Blvd.
Brooklyn 9, N. Y.

Dear Sirs:

We are in the market for plastic shower curtains printed with a flower pattern with matching window drapes.
What price could you quote us on two dozen sets?
Please let us know by phone or telegraph within the next two days.

Yours sincerely,

Abernathy and Smith
31 Rover Road
San Francisco 7, Cal.

Gentlemen:

We would appreciate it if you would let us know whether or not your nylon sportswear shirts and cotton wash-and-wear dress shirts come in size 16½.
It will be to your interest to give us this information as quickly as possible.

Yours truly,

Jones Hat Stores
Chrysler Building
New York 17, N. Y.

Gentlemen:

We are making a survey of the buying habits of American customers.

Could you let us know whether you have sold more brown hats or gray in the last year?

We will greatly appreciate an answer to this inquiry.

Sincerely yours,

Jones-O'Brien, Inc.
816 Little Bear St.
Chicago 39, Ill.

Gentlemen:

Would you please quote us a price on a gross of your 71 x 84 reversible wool blankets, 15% wool and 85% cotton, bound with rayon satin.

Very truly yours,

McGonigle & Johnson, Inc.
97 Duane Street
New York 10, N. Y.

Gentlemen:

Please let us know if your model 7B, 6 x 4 wash cloths come in pale blue. We would like to have this information promptly because we expect to place an order within a few weeks.

Yours truly,

Athens Box Co.
East Rock Road
Washington 21, D. C.

Gentlemen:

Would you be so kind as to send us a complete statement of the goods we have bought from you this year.

We wish to check our books before we get your final monthly statement.

Yours sincerely,

Manhattan Supply Co.
Laurel Street
Long Island City, N. Y.

Dear Sirs:

We have been pleased with your tabulating machine and we will want to order two new machines this fall.

However, we would like to know whether you are making a faster tabulator than your model V, which we have been using up to date.

Yours very truly,

Gentlemen:

I am interested in the service you have advertised for supplying temporary office help. We are often in need of typists and other clerical workers to prepare projects quickly. Would you please send me more specific information about your arrangements and facilities?

Are you equipped to have jobs done in your offices? Or do you have employees who would be interested in working at home? Are your rates standard, and if so, how do they run?

Yours truly,

Gentlemen:

Our firm is considering a move to larger quarters. We would like to find a convenient suite of four or five rooms, or of one small front office and a larger room that could be subdivided for five desks and a reception alcove. We want to stay near our present location downtown and expect to find a reasonably modern air-conditioned building.

Could you let me know what places, suiting my description, you have available now or expect to have soon? I would appreciate seeing one of your representatives if he could stop in to my office some afternoon.

Yours truly,

Requests for pamphlets or other items offered publicly need only identify the request and give adequate instructions for its delivery:

Gentlemen:
Please put us on your mailing list to receive whatever publication you issue on child care. Let me know if any cost is involved.

Yours truly,

Government Printing Office
Washington 25, D. C.

Gentlemen:
Please send me one copy of each of the following publications, as offered in your January listing. I have enclosed a check for $.60 to cover the costs as indicated.

> *Farming in the Corn Belt*—$.25
> *The Market for American Agriculture*—$.10
> *The Government and the Farmer*—free
> *Patterns of American Farming*—$.25

Please put my name on your regular mailing list for the monthly catalogue of government publications.

Yours truly,

Farnsworth and Gamble
32 Gladley Street
Cincinnati 3, Ohio

Gentlemen:
I am trying to locate a copy, new or used, of Mary Halsworthy's *History of Modern Primates*. The book was published by Smythe and Freddy in 1921, and is now, I understand, out of print.
If you have a copy and it is in reasonably good condition, please

send it to me C.O.D. If you don't have a copy now, I'd appreciate being notified, should a copy show up later.

Yours truly,

Editor
Homemaker's Journal
48 State Street
New York 17, New York

Dear Sir:

In "Recipes for Warm Weather," published in your *July* issue, your writer mentioned a non-fattening whipped cream substitute. I wonder if you could tell me who manufactures this product. Do you know of any distributor of it in my area? I have been unable to find it at our local markets.

Yours truly,

Sentences and Phrases

How soon can you deliver 500 folders of the same size and quality as the samples we enclose?

Please tell us if there is any special way in which you would like us to package the goods you ordered.

Would you be kind enough to send us the following information as soon as possible?

May we ask for the following data, if it is not against your policy to give out such information?

Will you please tell us

Will you kindly inform me whether

Would you be so kind as to inform me

May I ask you to inform me

I should greatly appreciate your telling me

May I request the following information?

I should like to know whether

I shall greatly appreciate it if you will

Are you in a position to know

Is it possible for you to obtain the following information for me?

ANSWERING INQUIRIES

The letter you write to answer inquiries should be just as courteous as the answer you would make in person. When you give information, you should appear glad to give it. If, for any reason whatever, you are unable to give your correspondent the information he wants, you should indicate your regret as clearly and sincerely as you can. The following are typical of the answers people like to receive.

North American Marketing Institute
15 Wisconsin Blvd.
Chicago 15, Ill.

Gentlemen:
Thank you for your interest in our firm.
In answer to your inquiry of September 12, we are really sorry to say that we cannot divulge any of our sales information. We hope this will not inconvenience you too greatly.

Sincerely yours,

Wool Furnishing Corp.
St. James Road
St. Paul 2, Minn.

Dear Sirs:
We are pleased to receive your inquiry for a price on one gross reversible wool blankets, 71 x 84, 15% wool and 85% cotton bound with rayon satin.

We can give you a price of $1440, F.O.B. Chicago.
Shall we hold these goods for your order?

Sincerely yours,

Mr. Leslie Roberts, Buyer
Sportswear Shirts & Pants Co.
Santa Monica, Cal.

Dear Sir:

In reply to your inquiry, we are sorry to say that our nylon sports shirts and cotton wash-and-wear dress shirts do not come in any size larger than 16.

We will send you our new spring catalogue as soon as it comes off the press, so that you can see whether any of our other shirts would be of interest to you.

Sincerely yours,

Household Furniture Co.
906 Driscoll Ave.
New York 9, N. Y.

Dear Sirs:

We are pleased to send you the information you requested.

Our Model 7B, 6 x 4 wash cloth does come in pale blue. We are enclosing a sample.

Sincerely yours,

Mr. Joseph Sellers
396 Madison Ave.
New York 17, N. Y.

Dear Joe:

The fellow who designed my prune packages is an old friend of mine, Stewart Johnson. He lives at 24 Jones Street, New York City, and his phone number is Perry 3-1931.

I'm happy I could help you.

Sincerely,

Mr. Walter Sutton
Sutton & Pratt Wholesalers
24 Teaneck St.
Paterson, New Jersey

Dear Mr. Sutton:

This is in confirmation of the telegram we sent you December 28.

Our price for two dozen pairs of plastic shower curtains, with matching drapes, would be $45.00.

Shall we hold them for your order?

Sincerely yours,

Mr. Jasper Means, Office Manager
Lead Pencil Co.
81 Pearl St.
Yonkers, New York

Dear Mr. Means:

In response to your inquiry about chartering three buses for your office outing, we are pleased to say that we can make arrangements with you.

Our local manager, Mr. Edward Smith, would like to see you tomorrow morning at 10:30. Will you call him at Jerome 9-2100 to confirm the appointment?

Sincerely yours,

Williams Manufacturing Co.
347 Cherry Street
Sylvania, N. Y.

Gentlemen:

With reference to your request of November 15, we herewith enclose a statement of your October account.

Frankly, you have put us in quite a spot. While we appreciate your wish to have a complete statement of the goods you bought from us this year, your request at this time presents difficulties.

However, if you can wait a few days, we will be able to send the rest of the information to you.

Yours very truly,

Robert Schofield Company
27 Allen Street
Seattle 4, Washington

Gentlemen:
Thank you for your inquiry as to the earliest date on which we can ship you 500 folders like the samples you enclosed. We can make shipment any time after Thursday. We are awaiting instructions from you.

Very truly yours,

Sentences and Phrases

We are glad to answer your inquiry. The only packaging requirement we have is that every item be wrapped in cotton to protect it against breakage.

We are pleased to send you the information you have requested.

Since it is not against our policy to give you the information you request, we are pleased to send you the following details.

As you requested in your letter, we are sending

At the request of your sales manager, we are pleased to

Here is the information you requested

We are sorry that we cannot determine

Unfortunately we are unable to tell

We have no way of getting the information you desire

SECRETARIAL LETTERS

Here are letters that a secretary may be expected to write in her employer's absence, or when her employer is too busy to write them himself. While any of the letters in this book could, with slight changes, be signed by a secretary, there are specific sorts of letters that a secretary is more likely to sign. These, for the main part, are letters of acknowledgment and "stopgap letters." (See the sections on these kinds of letters.)

Dear Mr. Jones:

Mr. John Rogers asks me to convey his regrets for not being able to answer your letter until the end of next week. Just now he is engaged in a complete reorganization of our Detroit office.

Mr. Rogers wants to assure you that he will answer your inquiry in complete detail as soon as he has finished this job.

Sincerely yours,
N. K. Slocum,
Secretary to Mr. Rogers

Dear Mr. Smythe:

Mr. John J. Hammond asks me to write you that he cannot see you next Wednesday at 3:00. However, he will be able to give you all the time you need next Friday at 4:00. Would you let me know if that time is convenient for you?

Very truly yours,
Katherine Rogers
Secretary to Mr. Hammond

Dear Mr. James:

As Mr. Fletcher will be in Des Moines until the first of the month, I am writing to acknowledge your inquiry of May 3.

I am sure that Mr. Fletcher will answer you in detail as soon as he gets back.

Sincerely yours,
Jane O'Reilly
Secretary to Mr. Fletcher

Chapter Five

LETTERS ABOUT
GOODS AND SERVICES

The only way to get exactly what you want is to be as specific as possible. This holds true whether you are actually ordering goods, or just inquiring about goods, offers, samples, or prices. You should cover all of these questions: *What? How many? For how much? Where? When? How?* This is your one and only insurance of getting just what you want, when, where, and how you want it.

You should give complete information about the following points, when they are pertinent:

Description
    Article
    Catalogue number
    Size
    Color
    Model
    Other specifications
Quantity
Price per unit
Discount (if for resale, or if you are given a discount because you
    are paying promptly)
Total price
Place to which goods are to be shipped
Means of shipment
Terms
Purchase order number
Date of order
Signature of person authorized to order

You cannot be too specific in the directions you give. For example, it is not always enough to mention a color such as blue if you are ordering clothing; you want an exact shade of blue, and you should state it. You should break your order down into the most minute details covering every aspect. It is always dangerous to assume that your correspondent will take something for granted.

There is only one exception to the rule of giving detailed descriptions of the article you order; that is, when you are ordering from a house that makes a single product. Obviously, if you are ordering packages of breakfast food from a one-brand cereal manufacturing company, it is enough to state that you want one-pound packages of that breakfast food, without describing the color of the box. However, when you are ordering a number of articles, you must for your own protection specify the one you want.

Let us say that you are ordering nylon stockings. Your requirements might be the following: catalogue number 35; size 9½, light beige color, 15 gauge—65 denier, full-fashioned extra long, reinforced heels and toes. Omit any one of these details, and you are likely to receive merchandise other than that which you had in mind.

Don't forget to include the catalogue number of an article when you are ordering from a catalogue, and just for an added precaution, mention the date or number of the catalogue.

Sometimes it is advisable to make shipping instructions general. You might ask to have goods shipped "the cheapest way" or "as quickly as possible." Usually it is advisable to be more definite about shipping instructions. When you can, you should specify "Via Parcel Post," "Via Express," "Via Air Express," "Via Fast Freight, Pennsylvania Railroad," "Via National Carloading Company," "Via Mercury Bus," etc.

Terms of the order may relate to the shipment when, for example, you order the goods "C.O.D.," or "F.O.B. San Francisco." They may refer to payment when, for instance, you specify: "2% ten days or 60 days net." They may cover the date of delivery when you write something like: "If you can make delivery by August 10, please send us the following, etc."

It is very important for an order to include both the purchase order number and the date of ordering, for purposes of identification.

The date should be complete, showing the month, the day of the month, and the year. The date, however, may not be sufficient by itself, since your firm might send more orders than one to the same house on some days.

With the purchase order number on the label of the package the recipient can readily identify the merchandise and arrange for its disposal.

In most firms an order is invalid unless it is signed by someone who is authorized to do so. This authority is usually vested in members of a purchasing department who receive the authority from the heads of other departments. In small organizations, it is usually the owner of the business who places his signature upon the order.

If you have occasion to make a great number of purchases you will find it convenient to use a printed order form. This saves time since it prevents unnecessary typing and covers all the requirements, which merely have to be filled in or checked.

There is one motto which should continually stay in the mind of a person who writes any business letter whatsoever, and especially one who places an order. It is this: *Always keep carbons.*

One prominent business man says that he keeps carbons even when he leaves a note for the milkman. This may be an exaggerated precaution, but there are many sad stories of businesses which have been thrown into considerable disorder because somebody neglected to make a carbon copy and keep it conveniently filed.

Always make out your orders in duplicate at least. Do this whether you use a printed order form or not. If your organization is large enough to have a receiving department, make out the order in triplicate. And if there is a special auditing department, make out a special carbon for it.

ASKING FOR PRICES AND SAMPLES

Brothers Hotel Supply Co.
1195 North Ave.
New York 2, N. Y.

Gentlemen:

We enclose details of our inquiry for dishes to be delivered before the first of next month.

Will you please give us your prices for the quantity named?

Yours truly,

Chicago Clothiers, Inc.
Morton Ave. & South Blvd.
Chicago 27, Ill.

Gentlemen:

Please send us samples of your lowest priced navy and black serge. We shall need 10,000 yards of each, with deliveries spaced equally over the next eight months.

Please note that we must have your quotation and samples by the 8th of this month.

Yours truly,

The Chatham Pen Co.
Reedston, Oregon

Gentlemen:

Please send us samples and your lowest prices for your fountain pens, model 464-B. Samples and prices must reach us no later than the 15th of this month.

Yours very truly,

ORDERING GOODS

Gillette-Burns Co.
411 Gleenwood Street
Cleveland 5, Ohio

Please send the following items to be shipped by railway express, and bill us. The order is contingent on our receiving the terms of 2%—30 days:

1 doz. linen handkerchiefs	.20	$ 2.40
4 pair tan pigskin gloves, size 6½	3.00	12.00
2 doz. assorted Orlon sports shirts	3.00	72.00
5 pair assorted cotton socks	.40	2.00
	TOTAL	$88.40

Sincerely yours,

Rogers Chemical Supply Co.
10 E. 22 Street
Omaha 8, Neb.

Gentlemen:

Please ship the following goods by motor freight as soon as possible, and charge them to our account:

15 lbs. bicarbonate of soda	@ .30	$ 4.50
1 gross boxes of aspirin	@ .25	36.00
20 bottles Rapp Syrup—#47 B	@ .50	10.00
	TOTAL	$50.50

Very truly yours,

Dodge Supply Company
Lawrence, Ill.

Gentlemen:

This is to confirm my telephone order of yesterday for the following items:

4 Jr. Sewing Machines Model 3A
7 Homemaker's Ironing Boards
15 Fold Up Clothes Racks

Yours sincerely,

Johnstone Company
Main Street
Verona, Mo.

Gentlemen:

We enclose confirmation for our order given your salesman on
January 12.

Yours very truly,

Men's Wearing Apparel
Linden Avenue
Maspeth, Mass.

Gentlemen:

Thank you for your samples of striped coatings received today.
Please make shipment in accordance with our Order No. 2602 enclosed herewith.

Yours truly,

Barnes & Barnes
Fruit Dealers
1930 Sheepshead Bay Rd.
Sheepshead Bay, N. Y.

Gentlemen:

Enclosed is a trial order for delivery June 22.

Please send in one lot complete, packed in burlap, shipped by
freight, New York, New Haven & Hartford, as indicated in the order.

Yours truly,

Modern Maid Fashions
25 East Tenth Street
Chicago 31, Ill.

Gentlemen:

Enclosed is an order for which we ask your special attention to time
of delivery. It is important that we receive these goods on the exact
day mentioned as we have extensively advertised the day of our sale.

Please let us know immediately if you have any difficulty in supplying the exact goods ordered. All orders must be delivered complete; no remainders must follow.

Sincerely yours,

Sentences and Phrases

Please send us the following items C.O.D.

We are enclosing our check for $234.56. Please send us the following items.

Will you please send, and charge to our account, the following:

We are glad to send you our order No. 475. Please notice that it gives full instructions for billing and shipping.

Please bill us for the following at our usual terms:

ACKNOWLEDGING ORDERS

Orders should be acknowledged immediately. Remember that when you acknowledge an order you may be making a tacit acceptance of conditions to which you cannot agree. A carelessly worded acknowledgment can often lead to a lawsuit, that is, if you carelessly make commitments as to prices, date of shipment and other details when you are not able to fulfill them.

The letter acknowledging an order provides a good opportunity to develop business relations. At this point, you probably do not have to sell yourself or your product, but you can develop the feeling that you are pleasant to do business with and that you care about your customers. Of course, an excess of enthusiasm or gratitude can be offensive. The tone of your letter should express confidence in yourself and your firm, but you can afford to show that you appreciate business.

Johnson-Thompson Co.
Waterville, Colorado

Gentlemen:
    This is to acknowledge your order for 15 lbs. of bicarbonate of soda, 45 bottles of cod liver oil, 1 gross of boxes of yeast extract.
    If we are to ship goods by the date requested in your order we can send you only 40 bottles of cod liver oil instead of 45 bottles. The other goods will be sent complete.

We shall be able to fill the rest of the order within a week. We hope that this will be satisfactory.

Yours very truly,

G. A. Barrett & Bros.
Hanover, Kentucky

Gentlemen:
Thank you for your order. We hope you will be fully pleased with the goods, and that we will be able to count you among our regular customers.
Please let us know if you do not receive our shipment within 4 days. We try to fill all orders within 24 hours of receipt.

Very truly yours,

The Stafford Co.
Wilmington, Del.

Gentlemen:
Thank you for your order #411 for 6 injector upset heads. According to our records, the price we agreed upon was $76.00 each, not $74.00 as stated in your order. Will you check your copy?
We shall hold the goods until we hear from you.

Very truly yours,

S. T. Goodman Corp.
Denver, Colorado

Dear Sirs:
Acknowledging your order of January 9, we regret that we cannot ship until January 23. Please let us know if this is satisfactory so that we can make shipment on that date.

Very truly yours,

SHIPMENTS AND DELIVERIES

Every letter giving notice of shipment should cover the following three points: type of merchandise, date of shipment, method of shipping. A notice of shipment enables the purchaser to check with the transportation company if the goods do not reach him promptly. Thus, if the goods are overdue, a tracer can be sent.

Newman & Newman
Opolis, Texas

Gentlemen:

We are very sorry to hear, in your letter of January 28, that you have not received the 20 dozen overalls you ordered on January 18. We have checked with our shipping department and have found that the goods were shipped by Santa Fe freight on January 23.

We have sent a tracer to the railroad company and expect to have a telegram tomorrow morning. If we cannot locate your goods within the next few days, we will duplicate the order.

We trust this will be satisfactory.

Yours sincerely,

C. P. Jennings, Inc.
Austin, Texas

Gentlemen:

We thank you for your order of July 7, which has just been received. It will be given our prompt attention. Should you find it necessary to write to us about this order, please mention our File No. 3189.

Very truly yours,

Sentences and Phrases

This letter notifies you that your order for 72 Bridge Tables, No. 188, dated July 7, was shipped today by Transcontinental Railroad.

We acknowledge with thanks the receipt of your Order No. 3127, dated July 10, for the following:

This letter acknowledges the receipt of your order of

This is to thank you for your order of November 10. It is being filled today. Invoice and bill of lading are enclosed.

Many thanks for your order of yesterday which has been forwarded to our plant for immediate manufacture. Delivery will be made October 5.

Thank you for your letter advising us that you have shipped our order for 10 cartons of Animal Food by Santa Fe freight.

FOLLOW-UPS

Last week, we wrote to you for some information about your Fall Catalogue. There is one more question we would like to ask.

Thank you for your letter of August 12. We would like the following additional information.

Have you received the samples which we shipped you May 4?

Before you decide where you are going to place the order you discussed with us, we would like you to look into the following matter.

This letter is to remind you that the samples we sent you represent only the most popular numbers in stock. If you wish to see others, we shall be glad to send them to you.

This is to supplement our letter of July 7. We neglected to mention that we can give you free delivery anywhere within the United States.

BARGAINING LETTERS

In bargaining, the buyer usually tries to show the seller that he is not in great need of the product, that the product is not worth as much as the seller says it is, and that the same product can be had elsewhere at a lower price. The seller must persuade the buyer that the product is worth the full price and that it is superior to all others of the same kind.

In order to be effective at all, bargaining must be carried on with as much courtesy as possible. Offending the other party would make it awkward for him to agree with you.

Ronald Drug Company
421 Swan Boulevard
Detroit 12, Mich.

Dear Sirs:

We have been very pleased with your product, as you know. However, we find that we can obtain a price of $4.00 per hundred with a local firm. This is fifty cents per hundred lower than your price.

If you can see your way clear to meeting these figures we would be pleased to place with you an order that will carry us for the rest of this year. That order is likely to be one of the largest that we have ever placed with you.

Yours truly,

Bryant & Cardinal
421 Maple Avenue
Minneapolis 2, Minn.

Gentlemen:

We are aware of the fact that your office equipment is among the best on the market. We realize that your materials are of the very highest quality and that you pay the highest wages in the field.

Nevertheless, we would prefer handling lower quality goods if we could get a lower price. Our customers do not demand the standard of quality that you put into your equipment. If we are to continue doing business with you we must ask for a 7½% reduction in price in order that we may achieve a higher volume of sales. We shall wait for a price from you before we decide where to place our next order.

Yours truly,

Rogers & Pratt
21 Fairfax Avenue
Boston 13, Massachusetts

Dear Sirs:

We regret that it is not possible to accept the reduced price you offer. It was very kind of you to suggest meeting us half way, but this will not be enough to compensate for our increased overhead and advertising.

Unless you see your way clear to grant us an additional reduction in price, we may have to discontinue our very pleasant arrangement with you.

Yours cordially,

Answering the Bargaining Letter

Smith & Jones Wholesale Company
95 Broadway
New York 5, New York

Dear Sirs:

Thank you for your letter of June 12. In view of the fact that we have done business with each other for so long and that you have bought from us such a volume of office equipment, we would like to meet you half way in your request for lower prices.

May we suggest an overall reduction of 4% in price, which will hold right down the line.

Since our own overhead has increased somewhat in the last few months, this offer on our part is good only for a few months. At the end of that time you will have to go back to the previous price list.

Our sales manager, Mr. Smith, will call on you with some display material which should help you to effect a higher volume of sales.

Yours sincerely,

Smith & Jones
West 24th Street
New York 12, N. Y.

Gentlemen:

After discussing the matter with our Board of Directors, we have decided we can comply with your request for lower prices. Attached is a corrected price list for our merchandise.

Yours very truly,

Peabody & Smith
7 Duane Street
Macon, Georgia

Dear Sirs:

In reference to your letter of May 7, we cannot make a better offer than the one we suggested to you. We feel that that offer itself is most generous under the circumstances.

In checking our books, we find that you have purchased from us twice as much the first three months of this year as you did in the first three months of last year. This indicates to us that you have been successful in retailing our merchandise.

We hope that upon reconsideration you will be able to accept our offer. We have been very pleased to have you on our list of accounts.

Yours truly,

O'Brien Drugstore
492 Little Elm Street
Syracuse, New York

Dear Sirs:

We are sorry to say it is not possible for us to meet the price you requested in your letter of November 9.

If you care to place an order with us any time in the future, you may be assured of the same prompt attention which you have had in the past.

Yours very truly,

Chapter Six

LETTERS OF COMPLAINT AND ADJUSTMENT

WRITING LETTERS OF COMPLAINT

Ordinarily, the purpose of writing a letter of complaint is to get better service. The more specific your letter, the easier it will be for your correspondent to handle your complaint.

Also, the more calm and considerate your own letter is, the better your chance of getting satisfaction will probably be. You will be helping your correspondent to deal with you without embarrassment. Usually you can assume that he means well. If you try to understand his position, he will appreciate your consideration and will want to co-operate. Sarcasm may make you feel better when you are writing your letter, but it probably can't help you make your point as well as calmness and clarity.

John Marshall Jones & Co.
94 Jefferson Street
New York 3, N. Y.

Gentlemen:

I am sorry to say that we are greatly inconvenienced by the fact that your goods are frequently sent to our receiving department after 5:00 P.M. Furthermore, your deliveries have very often arrived well after the time specified in our letter of May 12. Unless we get better co-operation from you in the future we shall have to follow the strict terms of our contract and cancel all further orders.

Sincerely yours,

R. C. Weathers & Co.
51 Pilgrim Place
Boston 4, Mass.

Gentlemen:

Unfortunately, your shipment of 10 Ironing Boards, received today at the Hartford depot (New York, New Haven & Hartford R.R.), is so greatly damaged that we are unable to accept it.

May we remind you that, according to the terms of our contract, we are to receive goods in perfect condition on or before next Thursday. Please send us your advice by telegram.

Yours truly,

The Green-Brown Co.
444 Elm Street
Scott, Pa.

Gentlemen:

We are obliged to return the shipment which we received from you today. This is order 47–8 dated March 17.

The china was so poorly packed that six of the cups were broken. There are shortages as follows: 5 cups, 3 plates, and 7 saucers.

We would greatly appreciate it if you would make good the damaged items, and forward the rest of the order so that we may have it for our weekend sale.

Very truly yours,

J. Walter Smith Recording Company
Bryant Avenue
San Francisco 9, Calif.

Gentlemen:

Twelve of the 150 records I ordered from you last Thursday were completely smashed when they arrived at the depot here.

I am enclosing a carbon copy of our order with asterisks after the name of each of the broken records. Please get them to us within twenty-four hours if possible, because our customer is very eager to have them.

Yours sincerely,

Oldtown Mfg. Co.
Oldtown, Ohio

Gentlemen:

We do not like to go over the head of your district manager, but we find in this case we must.

Your New York branch has made so many mistakes in filling our orders, has so consistently failed to answer our request for information, and has made so many mistakes in its billing, that we have been very seriously inconvenienced.

Since we have had such pleasant dealings with you in the past, we wish to give you this opportunity to correct the situation. Is there anything you can do about it?

Sincerely yours,

Acme Machine Co.
Springfield, Wis.

Dear Sirs:

The stamping machine we bought from you on May 6 is unconditionally guaranteed for a year. We find that the machine has broken down completely. We have had a mechanic look it over. He reports that the rotators appear to have been cracked before the machine was installed.

Since you have no service man in this territory we are obliged to return the machine to you collect. We hope you can send us a new one within a few days.

Very truly yours,

Beats-all Pen Corp.
Bigville, N. J.

Dear Sirs:

A number of our customers have been complaining that your fountain pens leak badly. As a result, we have lost a good deal of time and have been put to considerable expense for cleaning bills.

We have had trouble only with your last shipment of fountain pens. The ones we received before were most satisfactory.

You will probably want to check with your manufacturing department to see if there is any defect in these pens, and with your shipping department to find out if they are packed with adequate protection for shipment.

We are returning the entire remainder of these pens, two gross. We hope you can replace these with a shipment that will not give us any trouble.

Yours sincerely,

Everybody's Emporium
Detroit 15, Mich.

Gentlemen:

Somebody in your organization has made a mistake in filling the order I sent you last Wednesday.

I ordered a gray hat size 7½, Model 27B.

I received a green hat size 8, Model 31D.

I am returning the second hat, and would like to receive the first one as quickly as possible.

Yours sincerely,

Caslon Company,
Louisville 3, Ky.

Gentlemen:

Referring to your letter advising us of the shipment of our Order #8219, we see that although we did not specify it you have sent this by airmail express. Since we were in no special hurry to receive these goods, we cannot accept the extra charge. We feel that we are justified in subtracting this from our bill.

Yours sincerely,

Smith Brothers,
947 Maple Avenue
Newtown, Wash.

Attention: Credit Manager

Dear Sir:

Years of business dealings develop, of course, an understanding attitude about slip-ups, but we feel that in order to keep the records straight, we have to take exception to the letter received from you in the afternoon mail.

Three days after we sent you remittance in full for our May account, we received what is apparently your last collection letter.

Possibly your clerk meant to send us a gentle reminder that our account was due, but instead he implied that we were in for a lawsuit. We know you are not generally careless, but we would like your assurance that this will not happen again.

Very truly yours,

H. T. Brown & Co.
Milltown, Mo.

Dear Sirs:

Our agreement with you is that we are to be billed at 25% off the list price. There has apparently been a slip-up in the billing department. We are therefore returning your last bill for correction.

Sincerely yours,

ANSWERING COMPLAINTS

The customer is always entitled to an explanation, no matter how unimportant his complaint may seem to you. If you wish to keep his business, it is important for you to answer his complaint as specifically and as promptly as possible.

Since you wish always to make the best possible impression on your correspondent, it is very unwise to deprecate yourself or your organization. When you *are* in the wrong, admit it, pass it off, and offer a solution to the error as quickly and as pleasantly as you can.

No matter how indignant the complainer is you will make a strong impression by showing courtesy and calm consideration for his position. Remember that his position probably includes an imperfect understanding of yours. You may explain what happened, therefore, from your point of view.

Plaza Music Store
Cornwall, Calif.

Dear Sirs:

Thank you for your courteous letter dated April 27.

We were sorry to hear that 12 of the 150 records you ordered last Thursday arrived in poor condition.

We are immediately shipping replacements of those records.

We are also discontinuing the new method of packaging with which we have been experimenting. We do not care to rely upon it when it has failed even once.

Yours sincerely,

Timberlake & Co.
Girard, Neb.

Gentlemen:

We certainly will live up to the terms of our guarantee. If you decide to return the stamping machine you bought from us on May 6, we will pay for the freightage and send you another one in its place.

Before you do this, however, we would like to make another suggestion. It is possible that the mechanic who looked at your machine is not thoroughly familiar with its construction. Furthermore, we have a serviceman in the territory adjacent to yours who will be glad to come in, inspect the machine, and arrange for any necessary repairs.

If the damage is minor, this would enable you to put your machine in use within a few days. We hope this suggestion will be favorably received by you.

Our serviceman, Mr. J. M. Smith, has instructions to telephone you Thursday morning.

Yours truly,

Mr. Richard Millington
339 Summit Street
Cloverdale, Mich.

Dear Mr. Millington:

With reference to your letter of November 5, we are very sorry that we sent you the wrong hat. Your gray hat size 7½, Model 27B is probably on its way to you now, since we ordered it shipped on receipt of your letter.

The mistake, of course, was accidental. Your order was filled by a clerk who has had only a few days' experience. We will take great care to see that such an error does not take place again.

Yours truly,

Hood-Stetson Corp.
Jacksonville, Fla.

Gentlemen:

We are investigating your claim as to Order 47–8 dated March 17.

Although we have not been able to explain the unsatisfactory packaging and the shortage, we are immediately completing your order and sending replacements for the damaged goods. It is possible that the cups were broken in transit, but we do not wish to hold up your weekend sale.

As soon as we have been able to trace the causes, we will let you know. We will make every effort to give you satisfactory service in the future.

Sincerely yours,

Mr. Harold D. Noel, Pres.
The Noel-Richards Company
Garnett, N. J.

Dear Mr. Noel:

Thank you for your letter of July 9.

We have no idea that our New York branch might not be handling your account to your complete satisfaction.

We are sending a special field investigator to make a thorough analysis of the New York situation. Meanwhile, we will be able to deal with your orders directly through this office.

At present it is impossible for us to tell what changes we may have to make in our New York office. What we do know is that we intend to give you complete satisfaction, whether any changes become necessary or not.

Yours truly,

Pelton Brothers
83 Tenth Street
Boston 7, Mass.

Gentlemen:

When we shipped your Order 8219 by airmail express instead of by parcel post we were assuming that you needed prompt delivery of the merchandise. Although this inaccurate guess was made in your interest, we are willing to accept the extra charge.

Yours sincerely,

The Corner Store
Main and Madison Streets
Middletown, Md.

Dear Sirs:

Thank you for returning our last shipment of fountain pens. We hope that you returned them at our expense. We have just found a flaw in our manufacturing process due to the installation of a time-saving machine which we have recently put in.

You may be certain that our pens will be as satisfactory to you in the future as they have been in the past. We are shipping you replacements immediately. We are taking the liberty of sending you an extra dozen, at no cost, as small compensation for your trouble.

Yours sincerely,

J. B. Nosuch & Co.
Parkwood, Oregon

Gentlemen:

We owe you an apology.

The clerk who sent you our collection letter—instead of merely reminding you that your account was due—has been transferred to another department where we hope she will not be so dangerous.

As always, you are good for all the credit you need.

Yours sincerely,

John Jones & Son
Belmont, Mo.

Dear Sirs:

Thank you for returning our last bill for correction. We will certainly see to it that you get the usual 25% off the list price. We are very sorry for the slip-up in our billing department.

Yours very truly,

Mrs. Lincoln Jones
Bellows Falls, Vermont

Dear Madam:

We were surprised by your letter of April 4. We are perfectly willing to admit that we are partly to blame in the matter, but we cannot believe that our whole organization is as bad as you say it is.

Of course, we are sending you a new dressing gown immediately.

We hope you will be able to drop in and have a talk with us before you take your account to some other store. We know that we have served you satisfactorily in the past, and we are sure that we can do so in the future.

Yours sincerely,

Chapter Seven

LETTERS ABOUT CREDIT

ASKING FOR CREDIT INFORMATION
FROM CUSTOMERS

The first thing you ought to know about a person who asks for credit is: *"Can* he pay?" The next most important question is: *"Will* he pay?"

It is never a sound idea to take the answer to either of these questions for granted. Some firms can pay but don't; some firms want to pay but can't.

Luckily, asking for credit references is such a formality that most companies would not mistake your inquiry of their situation for a real expression of doubt. Even if you do have any doubts in your mind, it might hurt your business dealings if you were to allow them to appear in your letter.

Here are some courteous matter-of-fact examples of letters that ask for credit information.

Smith and Jones
Browntown, Minn.

Gentlemen:

Thank you for your order which was received yesterday. It has already had our careful attention.

Since we do not find your name on our books, we are enclosing a credit application blank which we hope you will fill out and return to us so that we can make shipment at the earliest possible moment.

We hope this transaction may lead to a mutually profitable connection between us.

Sincerely yours,

William Green Co.
Whiteville, N. M.

Dear Sirs:

Thank you for your order of the twenty-third, in which you ask that the goods be charged.

We are glad to have your name on our books, and we have opened a credit account for you. So that we may complete our records, will you please give us the name of some firm with whom you already have a credit account, or the names of any of our customers who recommended us to you. As you know, this is the usual procedure in opening a credit account for a new firm.

Yours very truly,

Mrs. Cleveland Jones
Green Groves, N. J.

Dear Mrs. Jones:

Thank you for your request to be placed on our books as a charge customer.

Your standing is such that we have placed you on our books immediately. However, our custom is to have two or more credit references in our files. Will you please send us the names of two or more stores with which you have charge accounts, along with the name of the bank in which you have a checking account?

We will proceed with your current order in the meantime.

Sincerely yours,

Bill's Stationery Store
Jeffersonville, Utah

Gentlemen:

Thank you for your order, which we received yesterday.

Since we do not have your name on our books, we should very much appreciate your sending us a check for the amount, or, if you want to open a monthly account with us, the names of two trade references.

Yours very truly,

Evans and Roberts
Moberly, New Hampshire

Gentlemen:

It is a pleasure to receive your order of September 12 for women's shoes. We hope that this is the first of many orders which you may place with us.

Your letter does not mention your method of payment. You are no doubt aware of the custom of the wholesale trade that opening orders are payable in cash. If you wish us to send the shoes immediately we shall be glad to do so on receipt of your remittance for $250.00.

Pending an answer from you, we have packed the shoes ready to ship. If you wish the great convenience of a credit account, please give us the names of some wholesale firms with whom you have already opened accounts. On receipt of these we shall be glad to enter you on our books as one of our credit customers.

Very truly yours,

CUSTOMERS GIVING CREDIT INFORMATION

When you are asked to give credit references, give them in as simple and polite a fashion as possible, even if you should think them unnecessary. Here are sample answers to requests for references:

Famous Manufacturers, Ltd.
10 Howard St.
Mason City, Iowa

Dear Sirs:

We are enclosing a check for the amount of the goods we ordered on April 12.

Here are our references: Rogers & Smith, Chicago, Illinois; Mammoth Publishing Company, New York; First National Bank, New City, Iowa.

Very truly yours,

Burns-Brown Corporation
331 Main Ave.
Cincinnati 21, Ohio

Gentlemen:

Thank you for your letter of the 27th. Since you say that you have opened a credit account for us, we assume that you are shipping the goods we ordered, and entering a charge against us for them.

Here are the names of four of your customers who recommended us to you: Continental Hotel, New York; Mayfair Hotel, Chicago; Travelers Hotel, Dallas; Abernathy Hotel Chain, San Francisco.

We have done business with all of these hotels for many years.

Sincerely yours,

Bright Shoe Mfg. Co.
Underhill, Mass.

Gentlemen:

We are enclosing our remittance for $250.00 to cover our order of September 12 for women's shoes—Order 24–8.

You are correct in assuming that we wish to open a charge account with you. Here are the names of three wholesale firms to which you may refer: Conrad & Arnold; Jones and Dupree; Manchester and Bryant. All of these firms are in this city. There should be no delay in receiving the necessary information from them.

Yours truly,

The Franklin Store
Chicago, Ill.

Gentlemen:

Mrs. Cleveland Jones wishes me to thank you for your courteous letter.

As both business and personal references I am requested to give you the name of Mr. Roger Fairchild, president of Marshall-Gold Company, and Mr. Oswald Brand, treasurer of Madame Irene, Inc.

Yours sincerely,
(Miss) Harriett Emmet
Secretary to Mrs. Cleveland Jones III

Moore and Hood
13 Peach Street
Baltimore 19, Md.

Gentlemen:

We are enclosing your credit information blank.

We would appreciate it if you could check up on our references within a week. We would like to receive our order in time for our midseason sale, which is scheduled to begin on November 14th.

Sincerely yours,

ASKING REFERENCES FOR CREDIT INFORMATION

Taylor and Anthony
778 Adams Street
Kansas City 3, Mo.

Gentlemen:

We have received an application for credit from Mr. Robert Smith who gives your name as a reference. Mr. Smith asked us for credit to the extent of $500.00, for a period of three months.

We should appreciate your giving us such information if you can, including his financial standing, the extent of his business and his reputation for meeting these obligations. We thank you for the favor of your attention.

Yours very truly,

Mr. Joseph Turner
149 Masson Place
Columbus 5, Ohio

Dear Mr. Turner:

Your name has been given us as a reference by Mr. John Christopher who we understand is a sub-tenant of yours. Mr. Christopher asked us to allow him two months' credit to the amount of one thousand dollars.

We should greatly appreciate your courtesy in giving us information regarding the extent of his business, his financial condition, and his reliability in meeting his obligations.

Yours very truly,

REFERENCES GIVING CREDIT INFORMATION

It is not likely that letters written in answer to credit inquiries would be seen by individuals of the firms under discussion. However, since there is always a possibility that the letters will be seen, the information given should be phrased with considerable care so that there can be no question of libel or lawsuit. If you stick to facts, avoid personalities, and leave out private opinions, you are very likely to be on the safe side.

Beane-Ford Corporation
New London, Conn.

Dear Sirs:

The firm you mention is very well known to us. They have very promptly met most of their obligations and on several occasions have discounted their bills.

We have not found them quite so prompt when larger sums of money were involved, however, and we are inclined to believe that they are trying to expand a little more rapidly than their present market easily permits.

Yours very truly,

Randolph-White Company
Denver, Colorado

Gentlemen:

We have occasionally had small transactions with the firm you mention and their payments have been prompt. Mr. John Christopher and his partner are hard-working, reliable men and have the reputation of trading well within their capital. We believe that you could safely allow the credit you name but we give this information without responsibility, and in confidence.

Very truly yours,

Allen, White & Richards
191 Woodward St.
Washington 18, D.C.

Gentlemen:

We are glad to be of help to you in connection with your inquiry about Mr. Robert Smith.

Mr. Smith's business is a small one, and we would be surprised to see him expand it very rapidly. We, ourselves, would not be inclined to allow his account to exceed $100 a month, and would preferably limit ourselves to that period.

Up to that amount we have found it possible to collect what is due us without much delay.

Yours sincerely,

Sentences and Phrases

The firm you mentioned in your letter is well known to us.

In answer to your inquiry, we are pleased to report that the firm mentioned——

is respectable and trustworthy. You may safely extend them credit.

is one of the leading firms in this town. Its credit is excellent.

has the highest standing, and an excellent reputation for prompt payment.

is reputed to pay very promptly.

meets its obligations with difficulty.

It is our understanding that the firm you mention——

is said to have a very small operating capital.

has a very low credit rating.

has the reputation of not paying until payment is compelled.

has lost very heavily on recent transactions, and therefore, cannot be recommended for credit.

GRANTING OR REFUSING CREDIT

Browning Brothers
881 Willow St.
Toledo 2, Ohio

Gentlemen:
   Thank you for sending us your references so promptly. We communicated with them immediately so that we could get your order to you by the time you asked.
   Replies from the references are highly satisfactory. We now have the pleasure of your name on our books. The merchandise is on its way to you, as requested, F.O.B. San Francisco.

Yours sincerely,

Wallace-Crane Co.
Stonington, Tenn.

Gentlemen:

Thank you for your letter of July 25 furnishing references. We are very sorry to say that they are not satisfactory.

One of the firms named does not know you as a customer sufficiently well. The other reference is quite unsatisfactory.

We are still holding your order, with shipping instructions. If you would please remit the payment we should be glad to send it. We suggest that you wire the money so that we may ship the goods tomorrow.

Of course, we may reconsider the question of credit some time in the future. In the meantime we trust that we can do a satisfactory business on the present basis. We are sending you our new fall catalogue.

Yours very truly,

Willis' Popular Store
Bryant, Texas

Dear Sir:

Thank you for your letter of yesterday giving references in connection with your application for credit. It is with regret that we report these references are not what we require.

If you will please refer to our last letter, you will notice that what we ask for are trade references, that is, the names of any firms in our district who have supplied you with goods on credit terms. We are sorry to trouble you again in this matter, but a house policy requires that we have trade references and not personal references alone.

When this routine matter is settled, we expect a very agreeable business relationship.

Sincerely yours,

The Lee Mfg. Co.
2041 Fulton St.
St. Louis 8, Mo.

Gentlemen:

Please excuse me for having given unsatisfactory references in connection with my request for credit. I thought these would be adequate, to say the least, since they are very well known in the business world. I am, nevertheless, pleased to be able to add the names of the following firms with whom I have accounts: Jones & Heffron, St. Louis, Missouri; Holliday Brothers, Dallas, Texas; Dunby & Son, Chicago, Illinois.

Please look us up promptly so that we may receive the goods we ordered just as soon as possible.

Yours truly,

ASKING FOR PAYMENT IN ADVANCE

Mrs. Washington Smith
Greenville, Pa.

Dear Madam:

Thank you for your order of April 9. We are sorry that we must delay shipping it to you. We are holding the merchandise in readiness to ship on receipt of your remittance for $47.00.

Since our terms are always cash in advance, we have no facilities for C.O.D. shipment.

Yours truly,

Mr. W. J. Brown
4140 Wall Street
El Paso, Texas

Dear Mr. Brown:

Your order for six jars of Health Malt has been received. Since ours is strictly a cash business, we cannot open an account for you.

Could you send us your check for $4.20 to cover the cost plus shipping charges?

On receipt of this we shall ship the Malt at once.

Sincerely yours,

Terry's Quality Store
Douglas, Florida

Gentlemen:

Ours is a strictly cash business and we have no facilities for sending goods C.O.D. We hope that the misunderstanding about this point will not be an inconvenience to you. We are holding your order for twelve pairs of boys' trousers, Catalogue numbers 4712 and 4714, pending the receipt of $60.12 to cover the cost and carrying charges. Thank you.

Yours sincerely,

Chapter Eight

COLLECTION LETTERS

Most business firms pay their accounts promptly, so that you don't have to ask them for payment. Sometimes even well established firms pay a few days later, and in such cases there is little need to remind them of their tardiness. If you begin to cry out for payment on the split second, you will give your customers the impression that you haven't much faith in them, or confidence in yourself. It is time enough to write your first collection letter when a few days' grace have demonstrated your courtesy, patience and confidence.

Collection letters are usually written in series.

The first letter is written just to remind the customer that his bill is overdue, and simply and courteously asks for payment.

The second letter is still a reminder, but it is a little more emphatic, tactfully urging payment.

The third letter, written after a considerable waiting period, insists on payment, and is very firm in tone.

The fourth letter demands payment, stressing the fact that you intend to collect even if you have to use your attorney or put the delinquent account in the hands of a collection agency.

Collection letters are one instance in which printed form letters may be more effective and pleasant than individualized personal letters, at least in the earlier stages of communication. Being impersonal, they permit the debtor to comply more graciously, without the embarrassment that is only going to increase the longer he waits. By embarrassing a customer unnecessarily, you may get his payment now, but you may lose his business in the future.

The following are collection letters which embody the principle here outlined. First we give examples of letters at each stage, then several series of letters that might be used in the collection of given accounts.

LETTERS THAT ASK FOR PAYMENT

The *first collection letters* are just reminders that accounts are due. While they are usually not sent out before two weeks following the due date, a longer time is frequently allowed to elapse.

(a)

Dear Sir:

In looking through our accounts, we find an amount of $8.00 against you for a January purchase. We are sorry to write you about such a small amount but we try to get these small balances cleared off early. Will you please send us your remittance? If you have already done so, please excuse our asking.

Very truly yours,

(b)

Dear Madam:

Apparently you overlooked your bill of $60.05 for items purchased during October. It would be a great convenience to us to have your check as soon as possible.

Yours very truly,

(c)

Dear Sir:

You have been so prompt in your payment of bills that we are sure you overlooked your January account. The amount of that month's purchases come to $225.00. We hope that you will find it convenient now to send us your check for this amount.

Yours sincerely,

(d)

Dear Sir:

$47.50 due January 12

May we call your attention to the above account which has probably escaped your notice?

As your account is a monthly one we should be pleased to receive your remittance in settlement at an early date.

Yours truly,

(e)

Gentlemen:

We find that a balance of $92.00 still remains on your account. We would be very pleased to have you settle it because we, too, have obligations to meet.

Yours truly,

LETTERS THAT URGE PAYMENT

The second collection letter follows the first one within two weeks or a month, according to circumstances. It underlines the request made in the first letter and is based on the assumption that the customer has simply forgotten to pay.

(a)

Dear Sir:

The amount of $8.00 for hosiery purchased in January is still unpaid. As you will recall, our bills are payable the first of the month following the purchase of goods.

Please disregard this reminder if you have sent your check within the last few days.

Very truly yours,

(b)

Dear Madam:

May we again call your attention to the fact that you owe us $60.05 for items purchased during October. You will be saved the bother of additional reminders if you can send your remittance in the enclosed envelope.

Yours very truly,

(c)

Dear Sir:

We would like to remind you again that the amount of $225.00 is still due on your January account.

Yours sincerely,

(d)

Dear Sir:

$47.50 due January 12

We wrote you on the 24th of January calling your attention to the above account, and we have not yet had an answer from you.

Your account, as noted on our books, is a monthly one, but we shall be pleased to extend this credit to a quarterly (three months) account which is the limit of credit permitted by our regulations.

Please let us hear from you soon.

Yours truly,

(e)

Gentlemen:

We realize that reminders like this are just as much an annoyance to you as they are to us. If you would remit your balance of $92.00, we would not have to write you again.

Yours truly,

LETTERS THAT INSIST ON PAYMENT

While the first two letters are polite reminders that the account is overdue, the third letter can begin to get a little tough about things. It should still be courteous, but it must certainly show that your patience is wearing thin.

(a)

Dear Sir:

Your January account for $8.00 is considerably overdue. Time and postage for the two statements and letters we have sent you have cost us over 6% of your account. Won't you please send us a check by return mail to clear off the small sum?

Very truly yours,

(b)

Dear Madam:

You have not communicated with us about your account of $60.05 for items purchased during October.

Perhaps you do not realize that we are willing to accept a part of the payment if you cannot settle it all at once. Why don't you drop in to see our credit manager, Mr. John Abernathy, whom we are sure you will find very sympathetic.

Yours very truly,

(c)

Dear Sir:

This is the third time we have reminded you of your January account. Your indebtedness is for $225.00, which is a large sum to carry this long.

As a routine matter our auditor has asked us whether we wish to place the account in our attorney's hands for collection. We answered that you have been prompt in all past payments and that we did not expect any difficulty with you this time. We hope that our answer was the right one.

Yours truly,

(d)

Dear Sir:

$47.50 due January 12

We regret that you have not replied to our previous two letters about the above overdue account. We must now insist that you send us a check for at least half of this account ($24.00) by return mail.

We are willing to wait until the first of next month for the balance of $23.50.

Yours very truly,

(e)

Gentlemen:

We were quite sincere when we wrote you on April 7 that we do not like to annoy you with letters like this. We are equally sincere when we say that we cannot wait very much longer for your balance of $92.00.

Please make an appointment with our credit manager within two days, or we shall be obliged to place your account in the hands of our attorney for collection.

Yours truly,

LETTERS THAT DEMAND PAYMENT

The fourth letter does not actually threaten suit. In some instances such a threat might be construed as libel. It merely states that you intend to place the account in the hands of your attorney or of the credit agency.

(a)

Dear Sir:

This is the last time we will write you about your overdue account of $8.00 for January.

Although it certainly is not economical to place such small accounts in the hands of our collection attorneys, we shall have to do so. We have a reputation for courteous service; we also have a reputation for keeping our finances clear. We intend to keep both.

Unless remittance comes from you in the nine o'clock Thursday morning mail, we shall ask our attorneys to contact you about payment.

Yours truly,

(b)

Dear Madam:

We have had to write you repeatedly about your overdue account of $60.05 for the month of October.

Apparently, you have not availed yourself of the opportunity to see our credit manager, Mr. John Abernathy.

We must insist that you contact us very soon about your account, since we shall not wait much longer before we place your account in the hands of our attorneys for collection.

Yours very truly,

(c)

Dear Sir:

We have placed your account for $225.00 in the hands of our attorneys for collection.

We have asked them to wait exactly five days before proceeding.

Yours truly,

(d)

Dear Sir:

$47.50 due January 12

As you have not replied to our numerous requests for settlement of your long outstanding account, we must inform you that, unless a check for the full amount reaches us by the 15th of March, the matter will be placed in our lawyer's hands for collection.

We trust that you will see the desirability of avoiding such proceedings.

Yours truly,

(e)

Gentlemen:

We have no formal collection letters which we mail out automatically at certain dates. We take the trouble to write precisely what we mean.

We have just discussed you in a conference with our credit manager and our attorney. Our joint opinion is that unless you remit within

three days, our attorney is to proceed to undertake collection. After
three days any correspondence from you sent to us will be forwarded
to him.

Yours truly,

SETS OF COLLECTION LETTERS

Wholesale

(1)

Gentlemen:

Ten days ago we sent you a statement of $36.00 then due. We
assume that you have not answered because you have overlooked this
bill, or because you intend to pay it later.

We have a large number of small accounts, and it is important
for us to receive them on the due dates.

Please send us a check by return post.

Yours truly,

(2)

Gentlemen:

Your account of $36.00 due on January 7, and we are sorry to
remind you that we have had no answer to our letter of January 17
regarding the matter.

The amount is so small that we hope you can send us a check by
return mail. This will save us the expense of further correspondence
and relieve you of the annoyance of receiving this kind of letter from
us.

Yours truly,

(3)

Gentlemen:

In reference to your account of $36.00 for January 7, we have sent
you two statements and two personal letters about this account and
we have not yet heard from you. We are sure you can see why we
will have to draw on you for the amount at the end of this week
unless we previously receive your check in settlement.

Yours truly,

(4)

Gentlemen:

You received goods from us on December 9. Your payment was due January 7—in the amount of $36.00. You have not answered the three letters we have written you on this subject. Finally we drew on you, but the draft has been returned unpaid. We have not had a word of explanation.

If you intend to pay but are unable to do so at the moment, you will find us very lenient. Please write us within the next four days and save us from the unpleasant necessity of collecting through the courts.

Yours truly,

Retail

(1)

Dear Madam:

This is to remind you that we have an amount of $27.00 charged against you for August purchases.

We like to clear up such items as quickly as possible. Won't you, therefore, send us your check within a few days?

Yours truly,

(2)

Dear Madam:

Apparently you have overlooked your account of $27.00 for merchandise sent you in August.

Perhaps you had intended to pay this on your next visit to our store. Since you might find it more convenient to remit by check, we enclose a stamped reply envelope.

Yours truly,

(3)

Dear Madam:

We cannot understand why you have not replied to the letters we have sent you regarding your unpaid account of $27.00. We feel that we have let this run long enough, and expect a remittance within a few days. Otherwise, we regret to say that we may have to take sterner measures.

Yours truly,

(4)

Dear Madam:

You are making it very difficult for us to collect the $27.00 due us. We have therefore asked our attorneys to take the matter out of our hands. They will probably not proceed for a few days. If you care to write to us by return mail, you might save yourself a lot of trouble.

Yours truly,

To Professional Men and Small Businessmen

(1)

Dear Sir:

I am sorry to remind you that your account is a few days overdue. It would be a great convenience to me if you could settle it within a few days.

Yours sincerely,

(2)

Dear Sir:

Ten days ago we wrote to tell you that your account was overdue. It occurs to me that you may not find it convenient to pay the full amount. I find it difficult to make this kind of offer because my expenses are heavy and have to be met every month. However, I should be glad to accept half of the amount now, and half within two weeks.

Please let me know if this is agreeable to you.

Yours very truly,

(3)

Dear Sir:

Even the largest businesses in the country do not like to let credit run more than a few months. I am surprised to find that your account is now four months overdue.

Frankly, I hate to resort to unpleasant means to get the money due me, which I need so urgently. But what else can I do, since my letters to you are unanswered?

Yours very truly,

(4)

Dear Sir:

I have not heard from you about your overdue account. A reasonable explanation of your delay would probably induce me to let matters wait, although I would find it extremely difficult to do so.

However, since I have waited so long, I have decided to enlist the help of my attorney. He has my instructions to proceed unless I hear from you within five days.

Very truly yours,

DEBTORS' EXPLANATIONS

It frequently happens that a businessman is unable to meet a bill on the day on which it is due. He may have had unexpected reverses; he may be awaiting a check from somebody else; he may, quite reasonably, claim that he does not owe the full amount for which he is charged.

A debtor almost always finds that his creditor is willing to give him extension of time, provided that the debtor makes known his need as quickly as possible and gives a courteous, reasonable, and detailed explanation of the situation.

Gentlemen:

I am very sorry that we neglected to settle our account which was due on the third of this month.

We have been in such a rush during our recent reorganization that we simply forgot about it.

We are enclosing remittance in full. We thank you for your patience, and assure you that all future payments will be paid promptly.

Yours sincerely,

Dear Sirs:

Thank you for reminding us that our August bill is due.

We had depended on a remittance to take care of this bill. We have had definite word that this remittance will arrive in two weeks. May we, then, request that you give us an extension for two weeks' time on our own bill?

Very truly yours,

Gentlemen:

Replying to your letter of April 28, concerning our account:

We are sorry to say that we cannot send you a check at present. Since the opening of our season has been delayed through stormy weather, our customers are still wearing winter clothing instead of purchasing the spring and summer goods we ordered from you.

It is likely that we shall have a change of weather soon which will enable us to realize on the present stocks.

We therefore ask you to do us a big favor. Will you take the enclosed note for sixty days for the balance of the account? If we have any considerable amount of sales before the note comes due, you may be assured that we will send you a check on account.

Very truly yours,

Gentlemen:

In reply to your collection letter of June 6, permit me to explain our position.

As soon as you adjust our claim to $90.00 credit for china smashed in transit, we will send you remittance in full.

Yours truly,

Gentlemen:

We have sent you three letters explaining that there is an overcharge on our bill.

Send us a correct bill and we will remit.

Yours truly,

ANSWERING DEBTORS' EXPLANATIONS

Debtors will rarely take the trouble to write to you unless they really do intend to pay when they are able to do so.

When a debtor gives you a reasonable explanation you probably will be willing to accept it, unless you can suggest practicable terms that are somewhat more favorable to you.

If you compel the debtor to sell his goods or other properties at a loss you may lose the opportunity to collect in full and you may limit the outlet for your goods in the future.

Here are answers to the debtors' explanations just given:

Dear Sirs:

Thank you for telling us that you are expecting a remittance within two weeks. We shall, of course, be happy to grant you an extension of two weeks on your account with us.

Sincerely yours,

Gentlemen:

We quite understand the situation which confronts you. We would like to point out, however, that if you had taken the weather into consideration you would not have gambled on your ability to settle your account on time.

You are such a valued customer that we are not going to insist on a full remittance immediately. We suggest, instead, that you pay one half the amount now. We will accept a note for sixty days for the balance.

May we expect a check promptly?

Yours sincerely,

Gentlemen:

Our claim agent in Hartford makes the following report: Whereas you claim that the china was smashed in transit, he finds that it arrived at your shipping department intact. We are enclosing the full details of his report.

This leaves the situation unchanged. Your account for $700.00 is ninety days overdue. We have had considerable trouble with this account. Unless we receive remittance within five days we shall place the matter in the hands of our attorneys for collection.

Yours truly,

Gentlemen:

We have just discovered the overcharge on your bill. Our accountant neglected to allow you the usual 2% discount for remitting within ten days last August.

We are enclosing a corrected bill and trust that you will excuse our error.

Very sincerely,

COLLECTION SENTENCES AND PHRASES

Accompanying Statement

We enclose a statement of your account for May.

Herewith is our statement for your October account.

We enclose statement for goods delivered last June.

Reminding Customer of Overdue Bills

We should appreciate your sending a check for this amount by return mail, as payment is now overdue.

You have apparently overlooked this item, and we trust that you will excuse our asking for a check at this time.

No doubt this small amount has escaped your attention. May we expect an early payment?

If by any chance you have made this payment in the last few days, please disregard this notice. In handling a large number of accounts, we sometimes fall a few days behind in our postings.

The collection of small amounts entails considerable expense. May we, therefore, ask you to remit this amount promptly.

Gentle Reminders

We wish to help our customers as far as possible in the matter of credit, but you must admit that your account is now rather overdue.

We could not possibly sell at such a small margin of profit if all our customers took the extended credit you have taken.

We must really ask you to give the matter your serious attention without delay.

We trust you will see your way clear to send a check by return mail.

Please excuse our reminding you again that you have not yet settled for the goods we shipped you last May.

Urging Payment

The attached bill shows an amount long past due. We would greatly appreciate an immediate remittance.

The account sent you July 7 was due at that time. We have reminded you of it since then, but we have not heard from you.

You have probably overlooked your account for $35.67 which was due three weeks ago.

I am writing you personally to remind you that your account of $275.90 is now two months overdue.

Several requests have been made to you for payment of the enclosed account. We should be glad if you would let us have a settlement, as we are eager to close our books.

This is the second letter reminding you of your bill of $36.86 which was due on June 3.

Perhaps you have overlooked the fact that your account for July purchases has not yet been settled.

We find that our recent letter asking you to settle your bill for $5.00 has not been answered.

May we again remind you of the amount due on your account?

We dislike reminding you of your account as much as you dislike our doing so. Wouldn't it be to our mutual advantage for you to send us your check for $3.00?

Insisting on Payment

We have carried your account for three months, which is considerably longer than we agreed upon.

We regret that we cannot accept any further orders from you unless you settle your account by return mail.

How much longer must we wait for a settlement of your account?

We should dislike having to place your account in the hands of a collection attorney. However, unless we receive payment within 48 hours, we shall be obliged to do so.

Our attorneys ask us whether or not we wish to bring suit against you for the amount of your indebtedness to us. We have suggested to them that they defer any action for five days.

Demanding Payment

Unless we hear from you within two days we shall be obliged to give your account to our attorneys for collection.

Unless we receive payment for the above in full by June 3, we shall place your account in other hands for collection.

Since you do not pay attention to our letters you may be willing to listen to our attorneys. We have placed your account in their hands for collection.

We shall wait three more days to hear from you. After that, we shall wait no longer.

If we must, we will turn your account over to our attorneys. It would be much pleasanter all around for you to remit today.

Our auditors have called our attention to your long overdue account. We can no longer allow it to remain unpaid.

Perhaps you think this is just another collection letter, and that we do not mean what we say. We mean every word. And we say that your account will be turned over to our attorneys within five days unless we have a reasonable explanation of the delay.

Debtors' Explanations

We regret that you have found it necessary to write us so often about our account.

Please understand why we have not found it possible to settle our account in full.

Will the following arrangement about our account be satisfactory to you?

Frankly, we have not overlooked your letter asking payment of $45.09.

With regard to your collection letter, we would like to point out—.

Your letter asking for payment of our July bill has just been brought to my personal attention.

I have pointed out to you that there was an overcharge on your bill.

When you have adjusted our claim, we will remit the balance of our bill.

Answering Debtors' Explanations

We are glad to have your explanation of our overdue account, and we would like to suggest the following terms.

Thank you for pointing out the overcharge in our bill. We are enclosing the new bill.

We are granting you a credit for $56.07 for goods damaged in transit. Will you please remit the balance at your convenience?

Thank you for your promptness in answering our letter of July 3. We are sorry that you are unable to remit, but under the circumstances we understand why it is not possible for you to do so. However—.

Chapter Nine

SELLING GOODS
AND SERVICES

The sales letter must first attract the reader's attention, then increase his interest, and, finally, stimulate him to buy the goods.

Your sales letter should start out with a short and dramatic opening. This can be a simple statement such as, "Prices are going up," "Water is more destructive to your home than fire," "Many women have discovered how to prevent runs in their stockings." The letter can also begin with a question such as "Do you know that prices are going up?" In this case the second part of the letter can answer the reader's curiosity about the question.

In general it is best to write your letter in short, complete paragraphs which make greater ease of reading.

Keep talking about the product and the customer, rather than about "I," "we," "me," "us."

The function of the close of the sales letter is to induce the reader to buy—in other words to "clinch" the sales argument. In most cases the failure to do this would be just like walking away from a prospective customer, saying, "Well, so long," before you took out your fountain pen and tried to get him to sign on the dotted line.

Make the closing of your letter short, clear and strong.

Sales letters can be addressed to the name of the recipient or to a general list, in which case they are addressed, "Dear Reader," "Dear Newlywed," or the like.

GENERAL SALES LETTERS

Dear Sir:

Have you wanted to be "an insider?"

Of course you have. You've longed to know the inside stuff that reporters, columnists, radio commentators, and others are not able to put into their regular stories.

Get back of the scenes with *The Insider!* A weekly ten-page private newspaper that answers the many questions you've been asking about Washington, Labor, Capital, etc.

Send 10¢ for the first 5 issues! You will be under no obligation to continue a subscription under our regular rates.

Sincerely yours,

Dear Mr. Ronald:

If we made this kind of offer every day or even every week we just couldn't afford to stay in business.

However, we *are* going to make it because we have such faith in our product that we are fully convinced you will want to order a full supply once you have tried it.

Our offer is simply this: Please accept with our compliments the sample of Etho Ink arriving under separate cover. If you are not thoroughly satisfied with it, keep it anyway. If you are thoroughly satisfied with it, quickly order any amount you like and we will grant you a discount of 50% off our list price. We will take pleasure in filling your order within twenty-four hours after we have received it.

Sincerely yours,

Dear Madam:

When are peaches in cans not canned peaches?

We are sending you a sample of our peaches in cans so you can tell the difference.

For these peaches in cans have the crispness, firmness, freshness, and the musky aroma that you enjoy in fresh peaches.

They grow in the Brook Valley where the rich volcanic soil is watered by little silvery creeks that trickle down from Mount Olympia. We pick them carefully by hand, clean them of their fuzz, and finally pack them in cans in such a way that they preserve all their flavor.

Try them! Compare them to ordinary canned peaches. And remember that our peaches in cans do not cost you a cent more than the other kind.

Yours truly,

Dear Madam:

I was driving by your house the other day and, frankly, your roof didn't look any too good to me. Of course I couldn't tell for certain from the road, and I didn't want to drop in and interrupt whatever you were doing.

May I come up and see if your roof has any weak spots that the winter rains and snow might find out? I'll do this free, of course.

Yours sincerely,

Dear Sir:

It certainly is an inconvenience to go all the way into town every time you want a shirt or some socks or any other minor article of clothing.

But usually you do go into town. You figure that no clothing store in a little community like this would have the quality of goods you want. Well, sir, then you do not know that we carry only the finest nationally-advertised merchandise.

We know that you will go to your favorite tailor for business suits and dress suits, so we do not stock them. But we do stock a complete line of haberdashery, sports clothes and accessories.

How about prices? We just moved into a low-rent locality near the station. We spend very little money for advertising, and as a result you will find our prices surprisingly low.

We expect a lot of people to come in and look around without buying anything the first time. We hope to have the pleasure of seeing you soon.

Very truly yours,

Dear Madam:

Have you been busy with paper and pencil, figuring how much you need to spend for your summer vacation? You had better revise those figures, because you will find it costs a lot less than you expect to spend a vacation in Holiday House.

Daily rates start at $10.00. That includes meals, golf and tennis, boating, swimming, mountain climbing equipment—everything you need for a delightful vacation. We are right in the heart of the mountains only four hours from New York.

We are enclosing our illustrated booklet and a list of distinguished people who have enjoyed themselves here.

Yours very truly,

Dear Folks:

We are having the time of our lives on Lake Gorney in Maine.

There are so many things to do you just don't know where to begin. You can sail the catboats all around the lake; and if you don't know how, Captain Billson can teach you. If you like speed, you can use one of the outboard motorboats; and you will feel as if you're flying. And if you want an all-day exploring or fishing trip, Captain Billson's brother, John, will take you anywhere you want to go, over to Green Hill, or up to Bangor.

Then there's fishing, hunting, tennis, and golf. We've got a fine library here, too. There are lots of games in the big recreation room, and the young people dance every night. Over in Warrentown you will find one of the finest little theatres in this part of the country.

We expected to pay a fortune when we first heard of Lake Gorney, but we find that it is one of the least expensive vacations we have ever spent.

Why don't you write Mrs. Annie Brown for the full details? We got your name from a friend. You are just the kind of person she would like to have.

Yours very truly,

Dear Sir:

We have found just the house you described in your letter of January 12.

This house has two master bedrooms, a large 18 x 24 living room, pantry, dining room, maid's room.

It's an attractive modern house with great glass windows that offer a beautiful view of the nearby Blue Mountains. The house is in excellent condition and comes with a half acre of attractively land-scaped garden.

Please let us know if you want us to open negotiations for you.

Yours very truly,

Dear Mrs. Bennet:

We've found just the apartment you've described to us, although, as we told you, we thought your requirements were going to be al-most impossible to meet.

You said that the most important thing was the view, and the view from the living room of this apartment is really breathtaking. You look down onto the Cloverdale Park in which you can see the famous Newbolt Mansion. The river flows just a little to the east and all day long it bears the traffic of boats going northward to the Sound.

And you can see two graceful bridges crossing the waters.

This apartment has not only the view you wanted but the little extra room, too.

We are enclosing a map of the layout. Note that the living room is 18 x 24 feet. The room marked "bedroom" is only 10 x 12, but it would be perfect for your husband's studio. The larger room, 14 x 18 feet, is usually used as a dining room but we believe it would make an excellent bedroom. The kitchen is more than ample, and has, of course, the latest refrigerator, electric stove and other electric equip-ment and improvements.

The apartment is very quiet. No traffic is allowed to travel on the street in front of the house, it is a considerable distance from the side streets and four blocks from the nearest train.

You will be amazed at the low rent, which is only $125.00 a month. We think this is an exceptionally good buy. Other apartments in the same neighborhood under the same management rent as high as $200.00 a month.

Please let us know if you can see this apartment within twenty-four hours because it certainly will not be on the market very long.

Very truly yours,

Dear Madam:

Many people get the surprise of their lives when they first sit down behind the wheel of a Royal Eight.

One touch on the accelerator, and the Royal leaps ahead like a jackrabbit, settling you comfortably back into your seat.

It is thrilling to drive a car with acceleration like this. But do you know what acceleration means in a car? It means rugged power to sweep you over the crest of the highest hill. It means speed to carry you steadily along the roads with the wind whipping your face.

"How I'd love to have a car like that!" we can imagine you saying. "But doesn't it eat up a lot of gas and doesn't it cost a lot of money?"

The answer is: Not on your life! The Royal is guaranteed to give you a minimum of twenty miles per gallon, and many of our customers report getting twenty-five to thirty miles to the gallon.

Furthermore, the price of the Royal Eight is only $1,800.00, F.O.B. Detroit.

Probably you have frequently passed the Royal showrooms at 112 Bond Street, New London, Connecticut. Why not drop in today and talk to our sales manager, Mr. Charles Curtis? He will be delighted to take you out for a drive. He will give you a thorough demonstration of the Royal.

If you decide that you just can't do without one of our cars any longer, Mr. Curtis will tell you about our easy payment plan.

Yours truly,

Dear Sir:

This letter will be dictated, typed, put in an envelope, and mailed all within six minutes.

Yes, that's a fact! All this will be done within six minutes flat by the stopwatch.

How in the world is it possible to get out a letter so quickly when, according to our surveys, it usually takes an average of 17½ minutes? All right, we'll tell you why!

This letter is being dictated on a Moderno Electric Typewriter. Don't get us wrong. It's not being taken down in shorthand and then transcribed on the typewriter. It is being dictated directly to the typewriter itself. Because the typewriter is so fast it makes shorthand a thing of the past.

We would like to prove to you that we can train any competent stenographer in your office to take dictation directly on the Moderno Electric Typewriter just about as quickly as you can talk. This means that the Moderno Electric Typewriter can be operated at speeds ranging from 80 words per minute to 140 words per minute.

Everything on the Moderno Typewriter works by electricity: letters, back spaces, carriage returns, tabulating keys. The touch of the Moderno Typewriter is so light that, if a large fly lights on the key of a Moderno Typewriter, it may imprint a letter.

How about letting us bring our machine in for a demonstration Friday morning? I will call your secretary and see if I can make an appointment with you.

Very truly yours,

Sentences and Phrases

In spite of rising prices, we can still offer you substantial savings on wearing apparel.

May we send you a package of our—?

We will pay just the same attention to your needs, whether you place an order of $5.00 or $50.00.

Only those who act right away can have the advantage of this new, reduced price.

Just clip the coupon . . . and watch for results!

We are as near as your phone! Just dial RE 4-6709—and we'll be on our way!

May we expect a trial order? Just mail the enclosed card along with $2.00; then we will send the machine at once. Try it for a day, for a week. If you don't find it suitable return it at our expense, and we will be glad to refund your money.

Try these at my expense. If you are not thoroughly satisfied with them, send back the ones you have not used. You will owe me nothing. I am sure, however, that you will keep them and will want many more. If you want any further information, please call ADams 2-7000 and ask for Mr. Smith.

Use these razors for ten days without paying us any deposit whatever. Then you are perfectly free to buy or return them. We rely entirely on your judgment.

FOLLOW-UP LETTERS

There are several kinds of follow-up letters:

Follow-up sales letters which are addressed to those who do not respond to a general sales letter.

Follow-up letters which are sent to old customers whose patronage you want to renew.

Follow-up letters which are sent to customers and prospects in order to announce the arrival of a salesman who will call.

Follow-up letters which are sent to dealers in order to enlist their help in a selling campaign.

Sales Letters

Dear Sir:

We have not had the pleasure of seeing you since we announced the opening of our new clothing store.

Perhaps you didn't think it possible that a store in such a small community could offer only the finest sportswear and haberdashery for really low prices.

Don't take our word for it; come in and convince yourself. To make it easier for you we are enclosing a card which will entitle you to a 10% discount during July on anything you buy, no matter how small your order may be.

Yours very truly,

Dear Madam:

"Inexpensive" is a relative word. What is inexpensive for a wealthy person might be very expensive for a person of moderate means.

When we say that you can spend an inexpensive vacation at Lake Gorney in Maine we mean inexpensive for people whose incomes are below $5,000 a year.

Just because we would like to add you to those who have stayed with us summer after summer, we are going to make you a special offer. If you spend a full two-weeks' vacation with us, we will give you the first two days completely free, including meals, sailing lessons, and a special fishing trip.

Yours very truly,

To Old Customers

Dear Madam:

We were browsing through our records the other day, and ran across your name. "Why," we wondered, "hasn't this good customer been in to see us for so long?"

It can't be because of the quality of our goods, because we know it's right; and it can't be because of our prices, because we know they continue to save people money day after day. You know that if you had any complaints to make about our service to you we would be quick to make adjustments.

There is a little bed jacket up in our Junior Miss shop that you would really delight in: Rayon taffeta in a full range of colors—and only $4.50. That's the kind of buy you've been missing.

Please come see us soon.

                         Sincerely yours,

Dear Madam:

We figure that the washing machine we sold you on May 7 must have saved you about 200 hours up to now.

We hope you are thoroughly pleased with it, because we handle only the finest merchandise in order to keep our steady customers satisfied.

Now that you are acquainted with the quality of our household appliances you might like to find out other means we have to save you the time you would like to spend with the children, or reading or seeing your friends.

Why don't you come down to our showroom at Maple and Madison Streets, where we have a complete model electric home? We think it is a very exciting thing to see.

                         Cordially yours,

Announcing Salesmen's Calls

Dear Sir:

Our Eastern Sales Manager, Mr. Robert McCarthy, is just about to begin his regular spring trip. He will arrive in your city on or about June 15 and will be able to give you a complete description of the office equipment we described in our letter of February 7.

Mr. McCarthy's headquarters will be at the National Hotel, where he will remain for a week.

We sincerely hope that Mr. McCarthy will be of help to you.

Yours very truly,

Dear Mr. Smith:

Since you would find it difficult to come to our factory we are doing the next best thing. We are sending our factory to you.

Our representative, Mr. Bill Hutchins, has been with us for fifteen years, and is familiar with every detail of our operation. He is bringing blueprints and a wide variety of photographs.

Mr. Hutchins is really more of an engineer than a salesman. If he doesn't think that we can help you solve your problems, he will certainly not try to persuade you that we can.

Mr. Hutchins will be at the Tompkins Hotel in your city from May 12 to May 20. He will give your secretary a ring soon after his arrival. We hope that you will find it possible to see him.

Yours very truly,

Dealers' Letters

Gentlemen:

After we sent you our price list dated January 12 we found it necessary to increase the price on Item JL-47. Therefore will you please change this from $3.00 to $3.20. We are sorry to trouble you and hope that we haven't inconvenienced you.

Yours truly,

Dear Sir:

Very shortly everybody is going to be talking about our Wonderflow Fountain Pens.

Our advertising agency has just contracted for space in three national magazines and in two leading newspaper chains. The total circulation will be more than 9,000,000!

This should make our Wonderflow Fountain Pens among the best known in the country.

We believe we have worked out some of the most dramatic and effective sales display material in the field. Our salesman, Mr. Howard, will call on you Thursday with display material. If you will work with us, we think we can really help you to go to town with Wonderflow Fountain Pens.

Yours very truly,

Dear Mr. Johnson:

A dealer over in Washington County sold $25.00 worth of our Peerless sun glasses in three days. This ought to answer your complaint that Peerless sun glasses don't sell.

We are enclosing a copy of that dealer's letter to show you how you, too, can really make money selling Peerless sun glasses.

Yours very truly,

Dear Sirs:

You've certainly made an excellent showing with our goods—so excellent, in fact, that we wish to help you do even better.

You have had such a talent for dramatic display and persuasive salesmanship that we would like to see what you could do with an even greater number of prospects.

Naturally the way we get these prospects is by local advertising.

Some dealers have been so excited about our goods that they have paid for their own advertising space. We don't want you to do that because we recognize that what is profitable to you is profitable to us and we want to bear a generous portion of the expense.

Therefore we would like to make you the following proposition. We will pay one-half of the insertion cost of any three of the enclosed advertisements in your local paper. The ads should be run any time between April 1 and June 15. If you can take advantage of this offer please write us at once. We will forward mats of the advertisements for immediate use.

Very truly yours,

Sentences and Phrases

Mr. Jones, our salesman, will drop in to see you within a few days.

If you have decided to try our product, you can place your order with our salesman. He will call on Thursday.

Here are some display signs which others have found highly effective.

We know you are pleased with the table you bought last month. Well, here is a bargain that will delight you even more.

You know there is to be a big convention of Elks in your city in April. How can you reach them? Here is the best way.

May our representative call on you?

I should appreciate the opportunity of calling on you to demonstrate our Supremo machine.

Chapter Ten

PERSONAL
BUSINESS LETTERS

The personal type of business letter should be used only when your business relationships are established on such a footing that such letters are perfectly natural expressions of your feelings. These letters are written to people with whom you have developed friendships, rather than to casual business acquaintances. Naturally you should adapt the tone of your letter to the person you are writing to, giving just the right degree of formality or familiarity.

GREETINGS

Dear Mr. Jones:

We gladly take off a moment from the business of buying and selling to wish you the very merriest Christmas. I am sure that continued dealings with you are going to make my own New Year as happy and prosperous as the New Year I wish for you.

Cordially yours,

Dear Mr. Francis:

All year round, I think of you as a friend rather than just as a business acquaintance. This goes double in spades this time of year when I wish you a very merry Christmas and the happiest possible New Year.

Sincerely yours,

Dear Miss Kennedy:

This is to tell you what a pleasure it has been to deal with you this past year. As a small token of my esteem, and as a way of wishing you a happy and prosperous New Year, I am enclosing a desk calendar. As you tear off each page, let it mark another step in our very pleasant relations.

Sincerely yours,

ACKNOWLEDGMENTS OF GREETINGS

Dear Mr. Wilson:

Thank you for your good wishes. In reciprocating, let me say that I look forward to a New Year of increasingly pleasant association with you.

Cordially yours,

Dear Mr. Jamison:

I am glad you think of me as a friend rather than as a business acquaintance, for that is certainly how I think of you. I look forward to seeing you again when you next come to town.

Sincerely yours,

Dear Mr. Studevandt:

Thank you for the handsomest calendar I have ever had on my desk. It was nice of you to send it. As a member of Hampton's Department Store and as an individual, I have always expected the very best from you, and I have never been disappointed.

Yours very truly,

LETTERS OF CONGRATULATION

It is always a good idea to send a business friend a letter of congratulation when he has done something that merits a verbal pat on the back. You might want to congratulate him for anything from winning a golf cup to winning a bride.

Dear Joe:

I was pleased to hear that you are now Personnel Manager, and I know that you are really going places. Your company ought to be congratulated for realizing you are the man for the job.

Yours,

Dear Mr. Oglethorpe:

Congratulations on winning the golf tournament. I knew you were a champion Branch Manager but I didn't know you were a champion golfer, too.

Sincerely yours,

Dear Mr. Jones:

Please accept my congratulations on your recent marriage. I was very pleased to read about it in the *Journal*. I'm sure all your friends in Glenwood join me in wishing you the greatest happiness.

Sincerely yours,

Dear Mayor Green:

Let me add my congratulations to the many which you are receiving. I am certainly proud and happy that you are our new Mayor. We can all look forward to a period of unusual prosperity.

Sincerely yours,

Dear Mr. Beck:

We have just been looking through our books and we find that your branch has established an all-time high for monthly sales of Super Radios.

This is to extend to you and your staff our very heartiest congratulations.

Sincerely,

LETTERS OF SYMPATHY

Dear Mr. Johnson:

Mrs. White and I send our deepest sympathy.

Sincerely yours,

Dear Mrs. Chartier:

I was deeply grieved to hear of your recent bereavement. If there is anything we can possibly do for you, please let us know.

Sincerely yours,

Dear Jack:

Although I am not a doctor, I am taking the liberty of sending you the following prescription:

Don't worry about your job—your salary or your work. Take things easy.

We look forward to having you back as soon as you can comfortably get around.

Sincerely,

Dear Bill:

I certainly was sorry to hear that you had to go to the hospital. The only good thing about it is that you picked a hospital near us so that we can drop in to see you during the noon hour. While you're away from the office we will send your salary to Mrs. Jackson. If there is anything you want and don't let us know about it, you will be fired on the spot. Take warning.

All my best wishes.

Sincerely,

LETTERS OF INTRODUCTION

Dear Jackson:

When I talked to you last Thursday I wasn't able to think of anybody who met your requirements. However, an old friend of mine has just dropped into town, and I think he is just the man you are looking for. Bill Smith did that wonderful sales campaign for Popular Salt in which you were so interested last summer. Enough said. I am sure you will be delighted to talk to him.

Sincerely yours,

Dear Mr. Chelsea:

Mr. J. H. Brown, who will present this letter, is a man I have known for many years. I have always considered him one of the most intelligent department store buyers I know. If there is anything you can do for him, I certainly will be delighted to hear of it.

Yours sincerely,

Dear Frank:

This letter will be brought to you in the hand of Elizabeth White. She is the young woman I told you about last Friday. You don't deserve to have such a fine copywriter, but I like to see able people get a break.

Sincerely,

Dear Mr. Thompson:

The bearer of this letter of introduction is Richard Roe, the son of a classmate of mine. He is seeking an opening in merchandising, and while I know that you do not have anything at present, I am sure that you can give him some valuable information.

I would appreciate anything you can do for him.

Sincerely yours,

LETTERS TO OFFICIALS

Anyone may, on occasion, have reason to write to federal, state, or county officials. Such letters should be courteous, brief, and to the point, and should always use the correct form of address.

Correct Forms of Address

THE PRESIDENT	The President of the United States
	or
	The President
	White House
	Washington, D. C.
	Sir:
	Dear Mr. President:
	My dear Mr. President:
THE VICE-PRESIDENT	The Vice-President,
	Washington, D. C.
	Sir:
	Dear Mr. Vice-President:
	My dear Mr. Vice-President:
THE CHIEF JUSTICE OF THE UNITED STATES	The Honorable —— ——
	Chief Justice of the United States
	Washington, D. C.
	Sir:
	Dear Mr. Chief Justice:
	Dear Mr. Justice ——:
	My dear Mr. Chief Justice:
	My dear Mr. Justice ——:
ASSOCIATE JUSTICE OF THE SUPREME COURT OF THE UNITED STATES	The Honorable —— ——
	Justice of the Supreme Court of the United States
	Washington, D. C.
	Sir:
	Dear Mr. Justice:
	Dear Mr. Justice ——:
	My dear Mr. Justice:
	My dear Mr. Justice ——:

MEMBERS OF THE CABINET	The Honorable, The Secretary of State, Washington, D. C. *or* The Honorable — — Secretary of State Washington, D. C.
	Sir: Dear Sir: Dear Mr. Secretary: My dear Mr. Secretary:
UNITED STATES SENATOR	The Honorable — — The Senate Washington, D. C.
	Sir: Dear Sir: Dear Senator —: My dear Senator —:
CONGRESSMAN	The Honorable — — House of Representatives Washington, D. C.
	Sir: Dear Sir: Dear Mr. —: My dear —:
GOVERNOR	His Excellency the Governor Albany, New York *or* The Honorable — Executive Mansion Albany, New York
	Sir: Dear Sir: Your Excellency: Dear Governor —: My dear Governor —:

STATE SENATOR

The Honorable —
The State Senate
Albany, New York
or
Senator — —
The State Capitol
Albany, New York

Sir:
Dear Sir:
Dear Senator —:
My dear Senator —:

**ASSEMBLYMAN
(LEGISLATURE)**

The Honorable —

Member of Assembly
Albany, New York
or
Assemblyman —
The State Capitol
Albany, New York

Sir:
Dear Sir:
Dear Mr. —:
My dear Mr. —:

MAYOR

His Honor the Mayor
City Hall
New York, N. Y.
or
The Honorable —
Mayor of the City of New York
City Hall
New York, N. Y.

Sir:
Dear Sir:
Dear Mr. Mayor:
Dear Mayor —:
My dear Mr. Mayor:
My dear Mayor —:

To the President of the United States

Dear Mr. President:

Your radio address on foreign relations should meet with the approval of all patriotic Americans. It certainly does with mine.

Americans may disagree on national policy, but we should all present a united front in matters affecting the prestige, power, and security of our country.

Respectfully yours,

To a Senator or Congressman

Dear Sir:

I hope you will support the proposed housing measure. I am sure that you appreciate the importance of such legislation. This measure is not only humane in that it provides healthful living conditions for the workers of the country, but is also good business because it will materially assist building contractors and workers, as well as manufacturers of building materials and supplies. But perhaps the greatest benefit of all is that adequate housing furnishes the right background for better citizenship and a more effective democracy.

Respectfully yours,

To an Editor

The Editor
The New York Star
New York, N. Y.

Dear Sir:

In my opinion the city authorities are mistaken in their judgment of where to effect economy in times of financial stress. The last place that should be considered for curtailment is education. And yet education is the first thing to be hit by our city leaders.

Surely there must be many political job holders whose services could be dispensed with, rather than those of teachers who have contributed so much toward the education of our youth.

No economy measures in the public schools of the kind that are proposed can do anything but harm. They will undoubtedly result in the unhealthy crowding of classes, with a resultant lowering of our present standards of instruction. It is not fair to our young people. It is not fair to us.

I hope that all public-minded citizens and organizations will exert influence with their councilmen so that the proposed education economy measure will be defeated on its final vote.

Very truly yours,

Chapter Eleven

APPLICATIONS FOR JOBS—AND REPLIES

ANSWERING ADVERTISEMENTS

The letter you write in answer to a want ad has to do a good all-around selling job for you. The safest procedure to follow is simply to set down all the pertinent facts about yourself. The prospective employer will want to know your age, your experience, your background, and your references, as well as the salary you expect. Be sure to remember that some detail about your experience which seems unimportant to you may be just the winning detail for the prospective employer. In general, however, you should show the employer that you will be good for him—because of your experience, your skills, and your interest. It is particularly important now for you to be neat, accurate, and pleasant, expressing through your letter as much as you can of what you are offering in yourself.

Here are examples of typical want ads:

ADVERTISING COPYWRITER—Must have experience on food accounts and ability to write hard selling copy. Married. Age 35. At least 10 years' experience. Salary open. Please write full details, age, experience, accounts handled. Box 27B, Herald.

PHONOGRAPH RECORD SALESGIRL—Classical and popular. Experienced. At once. Box 12. Times.

And here are example letters in answer to the above advertisements:

Box 27B
Herald
Dallas, Texas

Dear Sirs:

You ask for a man who has experience on food accounts. Here are the ones which I have handled:

         Holliday All-Bran
         Ryan's Mustard
         Miller's Baby Food
         Whimsical Wheaties
         LaFollette Milk

You ask for a man who has the ability to write hard selling copy. The two agencies with which I have been connected have made a specialty of coupon returns. On the basis of my record on these returns, I think I can demonstrate to you that my copy has brought results.

I am married; age, 34.

Enclosed is a record of my work experience.

            Yours truly,
            William MacDermott

Box 12
Times
Chicago, Illinois

Gentlemen:

In the last fifteen years I have been employed in the Radio and Phonograph Department of the J. Van Alstyne Department Store, selling both classical and popular records.

I would like to refer you to our buyer, Miss Helen McIntyre, who tells me that I have made an enviable sales record.

In selling records, I found my musical training of considerable value. I have studied piano for ten years.

I should be glad to call on you at any time you suggest.

            Sincerely yours,
            Louise Swanson

Here are further examples of letters written in answer to advertisements for jobs.

Dear Sir:

Here are my qualifications for the secretarial position you advertise. My stenographic speed is 160 words per minute, my typing speed 90 words per minute.

I am a graduate of the Interstate Secretarial School where I had training in many business courses other than typing and stenography. I am 35 years of age, and married.

I wish to leave my present position because it does not offer me the opportunities which I would expect to find in a firm like yours. My present employer, Mr. George Thurston (Vice-President, Jones & Pratt, investment counsellors, of this city) knows that I am looking for a new place.

The following are firms by which I have been employed in the past. You may write to either of them, or to Mr. Thurston, for references.

Southern Electric Corp.
205 Madison Street
Dallas 4, Texas

ABC Publishing Company
52 Third Street
Chicago 10, Illinois

I should be happy to call on you at whatever time you suggest. You can call me at BOulevard 5-9300, or write me at home, 73 Sands Street, Woodmere, Illinois.

> Yours truly,

Dear Sirs:

I was very much pleased to see that you are advertising for a bookkeeper because I have long admired your firm's work, and would have applied to you for a position some time ago were I not getting very valuable training where I am.

I think it is now time for me to take the jump. Here are my qualifications: I can keep a full set of books by double entry; make out weekly and monthly trial balances; make out monthly profit and loss accounts and balance sheets.

I also handle trade acceptances, drafts and notes and see that they are met on due dates.

For the last two years I have been with Smith & Jones, 21 Pacific Street, of this city. I have been in charge of their books all of this time, and I believe I will be given a favorable recommendation.

I am now bonded for $5,000.

As regards salary, I would like to begin at $80.00 per week.

If you will telephone me at SUmmit 9-2929, I can arrange to call on you at any time the following day.

Respectfully yours,

Dear Sir:

I am applying for the position as bookkeeper which you have advertised in the *Herald-Courier*. I have enclosed a copy of my résumé.

Yours truly,

SEEKING UNADVERTISED POSITIONS

Dear Sirs:

Is it true that you are looking for a rug salesman to cover your New England territory? I hope you will be interested in my qualifications.

I am selling rugs on the floor of the Jones-Smith Store. The last two weeks I have been keeping a kind of score. I have approached over 300 customers. I have talked to nearly 200. Sixty of those customers have either made purchases or expressed a desire to come back to the store.

I am not a super-salesman, but I do know rugs, having been in this department for three years. I have also visited a dozen rug factories, and have taken some courses in textile design.

Armed with that experience, I have been able to make an effective approach to customers. I like people; I understand people; I know how to help them pick out the rug that will give them the greatest satisfaction, and I have no inhibitions against exerting a little pressure when it seems effective to do so.

I know that there is a great difference between selling rugs on the floor and selling rugs to the trade. But since I have done well in the one, I believe I would do equally well in the other.

I am twenty-five years old, unmarried, and free to travel.

I will give your secretary a ring Friday morning to see if she can arrange an appointment.

Very truly yours,

Dear Mr. Hammond:

This is for your files. I know there is no position in your office at present, but I should like to be considered when there is one.

I am enclosing a list of my jobs and references.

Yours sincerely,

Dear Mr. Smith:

I know how difficult it is to get good reporters for newspapers in cities the size of ours. Either you have to train them from scratch, or you have to hire them away from other papers for more money than you want to pay.

That is why I think you may be interested in my application. I do know the fundamentals of newspaper work, having been for two years editor of my high school paper and for one year editor-in-chief of the *Athens University Journal*. I have just settled in Zenith with my family. I love this community and I would like to earn my living here.

I am not interested in using *The Zenith Herald* as a springboard to a job on a bigger paper. I would like to stay with it indefinitely. Because I have a small income, I would be able to start at $50.00 a week, and I would be perfectly happy to begin as copy boy.

I'll drop around to see you Friday afternoon after you have gone to press.

Yours very truly,

Dear Mr. Williams:

Someday in the future you may have need for a new private secretary.

Here is why I should like to offer myself for the job, and here is why I am so much interested in obtaining it. For one thing, I know that you do an enormous variety of work very fast and very well. This offers a real challenge to whoever works for you. It is the kind of challenge I like to meet because, with all due modesty, I have so trained myself in secretarial work that only exacting problems are interesting to me.

As to my mechanical abilities, I can take dictation at the rate of 180 words a minute, and transcribe at the rate of 100 words per minute, a speed which won me the Junior Transcribing Championship in Ohio. I taught at the Hooper Business School in Toledo, covering the subjects of bookkeeping, filing, billing, and elementary accounting.

I am familiar with your type of work because my father ran a small printing business in Toledo and for some time before I left home at the age of 22, I was acting secretary and treasurer of his company.

I cannot think of any job in which I would be so useful as that of private secretary to you, since, in addition to my business training and experience, I could put to work for you and your organization the know-how of practical, everyday business handling that I acquired in growing up in the printing industry.

Yours very truly,

REPLIES TO APPLICANTS

Dear Mr. Jones:

We were very much interested in your letter to us applying for a copywriting position.

Can you come in for an interview on Thursday morning at twelve o'clock?

Yours very truly,

Dear Miss Swanson:

Our buyer, Miss McAllister, would like to see you at eleven-thirty Monday morning, in her office on the seventh floor.

Yours very truly,

Dear Mr. Brown:

Thank you for your letter of April 7. While we are very much interested in your qualifications, we are afraid that you do not quite meet with our current needs.

We thank you for your inquiry.

Very truly yours,

Dear Mr. White:

Our custom is to have applicants for jobs see our personnel director, Mr. Slocum, before they are interviewed by the head of the book-keeping department. However, we are so much interested in what you have to say about yourself that Mr. John Patton would like to see you right away.

He will phone you for an interview sometime tomorrow evening.

Yours truly,

REFERENCES AND RECOMMENDATIONS

Dear Mr. Rogers:

The bearer of this letter, Miss Helen Jones, has worked for me for six years. She is one of the most able secretaries and bookkeepers we have had. I think you would find her a very valuable addition to your organization.

Yours sincerely,

To Whom It May Concern:

The bearer of this letter, John P. Smith, is one of the brightest young men I have known in advertising. His father was the well-known copy writer Roger Smith, and John Smith seems well on his way to establishing an equally high reputation in the advertising field.

Mr. Smith has a very unusual combination of qualities. While he is one of the most brilliant and entertaining writers I know, he is also capable of writing very hard-boiled direct mail stuff, and is surprisingly steady and conscientious. Frankly, I think he is a gold mine to whoever employs him.

The only reason I have let Smith go was because our billing has been cut down to such a degree that we can no longer afford to keep him. We let several older and more experienced men leave us before we were willing to dispense with the services of Mr. Smith.

Yours very truly,

Dear Mr. Brown:

This will introduce a friend of mine, Richard Roe, whom I hope you can use in your factory. He is one of the most promising young machine tool draughtsmen I have ever met. I know that you will find him intelligent and reliable.

Sincerely yours,

Dear Bill:

This is my secretary, Miss Jane Jones. She is eager to get into publishing, and I know she would be very valuable to a publishing house. She has been very patient with our rather monotonous business here, and I just don't have it in my heart to hold down such an intelligent and energetic young woman. I can recommend her without reserve for the vacancy you have in mind.

Yours cordially,

FOLLOWING UP REFERENCES

Dear Sir:

Mr. John Morris is being considered for a position with this company and has given your name as a reference. He tells us that he worked with you from 1951 to 1960 in the capacity of sales manager.

We would like you to write us, in confidence, of course, your opinion of Mr. Morris. We want to know what you think of his personality, his ability to get along with his subordinates and his efficiency in obtaining results.

We shall be grateful for your co-operation.

Very truly yours,

Dear Sir:

Mr. Smith has given us your name as a reference. We would like to know how you think he would be able to handle a position as copy chief in our small agency.

In confidence we would like to say that we are greatly impressed by Mr. Smith's copy and by his delightful personality. We wish, however, to assure ourselves that he will be able to keep up a good, steady level of work, and direct the work of others.

We would greatly appreciate having this information from you as soon as possible.

Yours sincerely,

Dear Mr. Dodge:

Mr. John Monroe has applied for a job with our firm. He has given your name as business and personal reference, saying that he has known you for three years and has been your private secretary for one year.

We would greatly appreciate a statement from you about his personality, reliability, adaptability, etc. We will, of course, consider your reply as strictly confidential.

Yours sincerely,

REPLIES FROM REFERENCES

Dear Sir:

In reply to your letter of January 7, Mr. John Morris was with our company for ten years. Mr. Morris, we thought, was a very pleasant person who handled his subordinates in a most successful manner and had a very excellent record of sales.

We can certainly recommend Mr. Morris very highly as a sales manager for any company in the field.

Yours truly,

Dear Sir:

Frankly I was surprised that Mr. Monroe gave my name as a reference. He was with us for only three weeks, during which time we found his work quite clearly below our expectations and needs. He showed little interest in what he was asked to do and, as a result, it often had to be redone. After the three weeks, we felt obliged to let him go.

Yours truly,

Dear Sir:

Thank you for your letter about Mr. Smith. We agree with you that he is a delightful person and that his copy has plenty of sparkle.

While we did not find him quite stable enough to suit our needs, it is possible that he will show more maturity in a more responsible position. We hope you can give him a trial.

Yours truly,

Part Two

SOCIAL LETTERS

Introduction

To put one's thoughts in a letter neatly and correctly is possible for anyone. To write fluently and gracefully is the result of training. To touch the heart of the reader, to make him chuckle, to make words paint pictures that transport another to distant scenes—these are gifts. But we can all express ourselves kindly, naturally, and in good taste. Our written words are permanent witnesses of our character. We can try to have the tone of our letters agreeable and appropriate. If one takes time to write he can make the letter an expression of his best self.

The model letters which follow are those of a family and their friends, people living in an average American community, traveling about as pleasure, school, or business takes them. The small boy goes camping; the young daughter is at boarding school; the older daughter marries and starts a home and a family of her own. The father and mother plan for the younger children, occasionally entertain for them, sometimes advise them—and at the same time they enjoy their own friends. Here are experiences with which all of us are familiar.

E. I.

GENERAL SUGGESTIONS

There are helpful hints for writing letters throughout the book, but here are grouped practical suggestions which the writer of social letters will want to know.

Writing paper should be of good texture, of a light color such as white or gray, should take ink well, and should always be simple rather than "fancy." Paper with rules should not be used, and envelopes should always match the paper itself.

Letters should not be written in pencil, even to close friends. Pen and ink are preferred, even to the typewriter, which might be used, however, for a long letter to a close friend.

When you use pen and ink, write as distinctly as you can, leaving equal generous margins and a good space between the lines. Avoid using inks that are unpleasant to the eye, such as red ink, or faded inks and others difficult to read. If you typewrite, use a good ribbon and clean type faces.

When you use stationery that is folded, write on the first and third pages if your letter is to be but two pages long. But if the letter is to be longer, you must follow the natural page order so that the reader won't be confused about the proper sequence of your message.

The address must be clearly written on the envelope, the letter paper folded neatly, and neatly placed in the envelope and sealed. The sender's address can be written on the back flap or in the upper left-hand corner of the envelope.

Understandably, personal or private messages should not be written on postal cards or post cards.

In letters to friends try to sound as though you were talking to them—avoid hackneyed and stilted phrases.

Suggestions for the writing of specific types of letters will be found in the following chapters.

These are the accepted forms for address and salutation to use in writing to clergymen and members of religious orders. The forms to use in addressing public officials are given in the first part of this book. (See *Index.*)

FORMS OF ADDRESS

For:

BISHOP (Episcopalian)	Right Reverend Charles P. Schyler 64 Lincoln Drive Milwaukee 2, Wisconsin

Right Reverend:
Dear Sir:
or My dear Bishop,

MONSIGNOR	Right Reverend Timothy K. Flannigan 45 East Seventh Street Valley City, North Dakota

Dear Monsignor:
or Dear Monsignor Flannigan,

BISHOP (Roman Catholic)	Most Reverend Samuel Winton 28 East Shore Drive Milwaukee 7, Wisconsin

Your Excellency:
or My dear Bishop Winton,

PRIEST	Reverend Terence Riordon 17166 Hayne Avenue Chicago 39, Illinois

Dear Reverend Father:
or Dear Father Riordon,

OTHER CLERGYMEN	Dr. Thomas P. Lawton 100 Gorham Street Madison 2, Wisconsin

My dear Dr. Lawton,
or Dear Dr. Lawton,

Mr. Henry L. Halsey
250 Menona Avenue
Madison 3, Wisconsin

My dear Mr. Halsey,

RABBI

Rabbi Stephen Winefeld
415 Bergman Street
Eau Claire, Wisconsin

Dear Sir:
or Dear Rabbi Winefeld,
or Dear Dr. Winefeld,

SUPERIOR OF A
SISTERHOOD

Mother St. Anaclet, Superior
Notre Dame des Bois
Trenton, New Jersey

Dear Mother St. Anaclet,

SISTER

Sister Patricia Ann
St. Joseph's Convent
Adrian, Michigan

Dear Sister Patricia Ann,

Chapter Thirteen

INVITATIONS AND ANNOUNCEMENTS

After the Christmas season with its many activities primarily for her family, Mrs. John Colan Hobart plans to entertain some of her friends—some formally, some informally.

LUNCHEON

For a formal luncheon, a hostess writes her invitation on her best note paper and sends it out about ten days before the date set for the luncheon:

Mrs. John Colan Hobart
requests the pleasure of your company
at luncheon, on Wednesday, January the fourteenth
at one o'clock
The Willows
3o9 River Avenue

The invitation may have the line, *To meet Miss Carey of Prairie du Chien,* or some other statement of purpose, written at the bottom of the page.

Mrs. Hobart has included in her invitation the name of her home, as is customary in many localities, and her street address, since she presumably is writing to a friend who is not familiar with it. For one who is, she might merely write "The Willows," to indicate that the luncheon will be at her home. If her stationery is printed with her address and "The Willows," repetition of them would not be necessary. Many women have their name, address, and even phone number printed on their stationery. Some prefer having only an attractive monogram, preferably in a dark, conservative ink.

An invitation to luncheon may be extended by writing beneath the name on one's visiting card:

Mrs. John Colan Hobart

Luncheon at one o'clock
Wednesday, January the fourteenth

An informal note of invitation can be worded this way and written on informal note paper:

Dear Mrs. Russell,
How good that you have planned to stay on here after the holidays! I am having a small luncheon here on Wednesday, the fourteenth, at one o'clock, and I do hope you can come.

Sincerely yours,
Janet Hobart

The Willows
309 River Avenue
January fourth

Dear Elizabeth,
Mary Holmes of Rockford is coming to stay with me a few days next week. She and I are both hoping you can come to a luncheon here Wednesday, the fourteenth, at one o'clock.

Fondly,
Janet

January 4

The responses will be in keeping with the wording of the invitation:

Mrs. Lyman Holcombe
accepts with pleasure the kind invitation
of
Mrs. John Colan Hobart
for luncheon on Wednesday, the fourteenth of January
at one o'clock

The reply to the invitation written on the visiting card is written on note paper. The reply to the note is naturally a note.

Dear Janet,
    I shall be delighted to have luncheon with you on Wednesday at one o'clock to see Mary Holmes again.

Sincerely yours,
Elizabeth Holmes

An informal note paper can be a small double card folded along the top and printed with the name: *Mrs. John Colan Hobart.* An "informal" also may be embellished on its front fold with figures such as flowers, kittens, boats, ducks, or cocker spaniels. These gay, colorful "informals" are quite acceptable for friendly, short notes, but you must remember when becoming enchanted in a stationery store with a box of frisky poodles, that your stationery represents *you.*

DINNER

To reply to a dinner invitation, the guest uses the same type of wording she found in the invitation. If the invitation read: "Mr. and Mrs. John Colan Hobart request the pleasure," etc., then she will reply in the third person:

Mr. and Mrs.——
accept with pleasure
Mr. and Mrs. John Colan Hobart's kind invitation
for dinner
on Saturday, January nineteenth
at seven o'clock

or:

Mr. and Mrs.——
regret that a previous engagement
prevents their acceptance of
Mr. and Mrs. John Colan Hobart's kind invitation
to dinner
on Saturday, the nineteenth of January
at seven o'clock

To the more informal note one replies:

Dear Mrs. Hobart,
We shall both be delighted to accept your kind invitation to dinner on Saturday, the nineteenth, at seven-thirty.

Very sincerely,
Hannah Latimer

If a dinner must be canceled, the hostess will notify her guests at once:

Mr. and Mrs. John Colan Hobart regret that, owing to the illness of Mr. Hobart, their dinner, arranged for next Saturday, must be postponed for the time being.

January 17

The note may be more informal:

My dear Mrs. Latimer:
It is with great regret that I must write to tell you our dinner, planned for the nineteenth, must be postponed until the twenty-sixth. One of our cousins from England will be going through Chicago on his way to San Francisco. He has wired us to meet him on the twentieth. I hope that you and Mr. Latimer can come instead on the twenty-sixth at seven o'clock.

Sincerely yours,
Janet Hobart

January 17

If a person must fill a place at a dinner party at the last moment, the hostess must be very gracious in her informal note to a tried and true friend.

Dear Gerald,
If you are free tomorrow, the fifteenth, will you join a dinner party that has been suddenly upset by the illness of one of my guests? I hope you can overlook the informality of this hurried invitation and

make John and me very happy by accepting it. We shall dine at six-thirty in order to be on time for the concert given by the University Glee Club.

Most sincerely yours,
Janet Hobart

January 14

A person who cannot accept a last minute invitation to fill in at dinner responds promptly by note and gives a reason for not accepting. The note should be brief.

Dear Janet,

I am really very sorry I cannot help you make up the number at your dinner party tomorrow night. I have a previous engagement in Milwaukee which, unfortunately, I cannot break.

Sincerely yours,
Gerald Brewer

An engraved invitation is printed on an unadorned card; a written one will be on the type of initialed or note paper the hostess usually uses.

Sometimes the invitation is a brief written note. Such a note does not imply that the dinner is informal. It contains merely the invitation.

Dear Mrs. Latimer,

John and I would be very happy if you and Mr. Latimer could come to dinner on Saturday the nineteenth at seven o'clock. We do hope you can join us.

Sincerely yours,
Janet Hobart

January 5

My dear Miss Thompson,

John and I are wondering if you can dine with us on Tuesday, the fifteenth, at half-past six. Afterward, we plan to hear the University Glee Club at the Auditorium.

I hope that you will be able to come.

Most sincerely,
Janet Hobart

February first

My dear Mrs. Hobart,

We both deeply regret that we are not able to accept your kind invitation for dinner on the nineteenth. I have an appointment for that evening to speak at the P.T.A. Richard joins me in kind regards.

Most sincerely yours,
Hannah Latimer

The note paper is folded once into an envelope, which is addressed to Mrs. Hobart.

When a guest who has accepted a dinner invitation finds that he cannot, because of unavoidable circumstances, be present, he or she must write immediately on note paper to explain.

Dear Janet,

Your dinner party of the nineteenth sounded so pleasant, and now I find, suddenly, that I cannot come. Little Tom has acquired some sort of virus that has made constant care necessary for at least eight more days, the Doctor says. Tom's a good patient and is already responding to treatment, so it's just a matter of time. But I am so sorry the time had to be right now.

Yours affectionately,
Sue

January 15

Hostesses who entertain frequently sometimes have their formal dinner invitations engraved with blanks to be filled in thus:

Mr. and Mrs. John Colan Hobart
request the pleasure of

company at dinner
on   , the   of
at   o'clock
The Willows

However, this would constitute a luxury for most hostesses. Invitations can be written quite correctly by hand, with the same spacing. If the dinner is being given in honor of a friend, the line, *To meet Mr. and Mrs. C. K. Foster of Platteville,* may be centered at the bottom of the invitation.

THEATER, OPERA, FOOTBALL GAME

An invitation to a theater party is usually written in note form:

Dear Mrs. Hobart,

Can you and Mr. Hobart join us and a few other friends on Monday evening, February tenth, for dinner? Later we plan to go to the Bernhardt Theater to see Burton Thorpe in *Hamlet.* Dinner will be at six-thirty to allow plenty of time for the drive into town and arrival before curtain time. We do hope you can come!

Yours sincerely,
Patricia Marks

410 Forest Avenue
Oak Park
January 26

Mrs. Hobart responds promptly:

The Willows
January 27

Dear Mrs. Marks,

We shall be delighted to come to dinner on Monday evening, February tenth. I understand Burton Thorpe is magnificent in *Hamlet,* and we are looking forward to the performance.

Sincerely,
Janet Hobart

Mrs. Marks' daughter, a music-lover, is invited by a young man to the opera:

1210 Lake Park
Radleigh
February 2

Dear Pat,

The papers say that Anita Giovanni will be singing *Tosca* at the Auditorium, Monday evening, the seventeenth. Bill Hanson and Gretchen are going, and we all should like you to join us to explain the finer points of opera! Hoping you can,

Sincerely,
Richard Barnes

One of the Delevan girls is at boarding school in New York state. She is invited to see a football game.

Kemper School
Danbury, Connecticut
October 1

Dear Helene,

I should like very much to take you to the Army-Columbia game at West Point the twenty-eighth of this month. If you are free to go, Mother will write your mother to request permission from the authorities of your school. Dad and Mother will pick me up early in the morning and we shall all call for you about ten-thirty. That will allow us plenty of time for luncheon and to take a look at the Academy before the kick-off.

Sincerely yours,
Grant Short

Saint Mary's Hall
Shrub Oak, N. Y.
October 9

Dear Grant,

I should love to see an Army game! My mother is willing that I go; so if the red tape starts rolling soon, perhaps I can have permission to be away from school on the twenty-eighth. I hope the Army mule will really kick up his heels.

Sincerely yours,
Helene

FORMAL AND INFORMAL DANCES

Formal invitations for a dancing party can be engraved on large white cards, or written on fine, plain paper.

> *Mr. and Mrs. John Colan Hobart*
> *request the pleasure of your company*
> *at the Lake Ripley Country Club*
> *on Friday evening, January the twenty-fifth*
> *at ten o'clock*

Dancing

R.S.V.P. to
The Willows

The replies are in the same manner as the invitation. They are written on a double note sheet, sealed and sent to Mrs. John Colan Hobart.

> Mr. and Mrs. Myron Care Grant
> accept with pleasure the
> kind invitation of
> Mr. and Mrs. John Colan Hobart for
> Friday evening, January the twenty-fifth
> at ten o'clock

10 Walworth Avenue

> Mr. Alfred M. Simms
> regrets that his absence from town
> makes him unable to accept the kind invitation of
> Mr. and Mrs. John Colan Hobart for
> Friday evening, January the twenty-fifth
> at ten o'clock

1050 Kent Parkway

Often, for informal entertaining, invitations may be made on a visiting card, usually a "joint" card printed with the names of the host and hostess. Date, type of party, and *R.S.V.P.* are added by hand.

> *Mr. and Mrs. John Colan Hobart*
> Dancing at ten.　　　　January the twenty-fifth.
> R.S.V.P.

A folded informal card printed with *Mr. and Mrs. etc.* can be used the same way. If the host and hostess want to make their invitation less formal they draw a line through "Mr. and Mrs. John Colan Hobart" and handwrite "John and Janet."

The hostess may use her card with only her name on it in this way when she is entertaining. Such invitations are commonly used for luncheons, teas, buffet suppers, informal dinners, and cocktail parties.

Clever, illustrated cocktail invitations abound at stationery stores with blanks for name, address, date and time. These are often used when a large, informal gathering is planned.

A personal note can be a more pleasant and simple way of asking guests to a party or dance.

The Willows

Dear Sandra,

On next week Monday, the fourteenth, we should like to have you as our guest to help Ruth enjoy her birthday. We are going to have dancing from nine-thirty to midnight.

Sincerely yours,
Janet Hobart

The Willows

Dear Michael,

In honor of Ruth's birthday, next Monday, the fourteenth, we are inviting a few of her friends to a dance from nine-thirty until midnight. We shall be happy to have you join us.

Very sincerely yours,
Janet Hobart

An Easter vacation brings two girls home from school. Their mothers plan a dance at the Country Club:

Mrs. John C. Hobart and Mrs. Clyde K. Ring
Miss Ruth Hobart
Miss Mary Ring
request the pleasure of your company
at a dance
on Friday evening, April twenty-sixth
at ten o'clock
at the Lake Ripley Country Club

Formal

Mrs. Hobart will enclose her visiting card in her share of the invitations and Mrs. Ring likewise, each indicating where a reply should be sent. *R.S.V.P., The Willows, 309 River Avenue,* will be added to Mrs. Hobart's cards, and Mrs. Ring will give her address in a similar manner.

For a charity or civic ball, the following form may be used:

> *The honor of your company*
> *is requested by the*
> *members of the Ripley Women's Committee*
> *at the Lake Ripley Country Club*
> *on Monday, April the twenty-ninth*
> *at ten o'clock*

Dancing

> *R.S.V.P. to*
> *Mrs. R. N. Latimer*
> *at 50 South Main Street*

ENGAGEMENT

Announcement

The engagement of a daughter may be announced formally in an imaginative way. Each guest at a luncheon may find in the fold of the napkin, or on the dessert plate, an envelope containing a card with the following:

> *Mr. and Mrs. John Colan Hobart*
> *have the honor to announce*
> *the engagement of their daughter*
> *Joan*
> *to Mr. John Francis Lacerte*

A more informal announcement can be made on cards fastened at the end of ribbons peeking from a centerpiece. The guests at some time during the luncheon will draw the ribbons. A variety of delightful plans can be worked out by brides-to-be.

Good Wishes and Congratulations

Letters from absent friends pour in after the announcement. The girl receives the good wishes, the young man the congratulations.

3204 Ontario Street
Oak Park, Illinois
March 1, 19

My dear Joan,

The clipping from *The Delevan Gazette* that your mother enclosed in her last letter told me of your approaching marriage. My very best love to you, my dear, and the heartiest congratulations to the fortunate Mr. Lacerte. Your progress from toddler days has always been of great interest to me even though we haven't seen each other often. Your mother and I laid great plans for you even before you were born. I hope you will find use for the little token of good will I'm mailing you. It carries much love with it.

Affectionately,
Janet McKenzie

Dear Joan,

What an occasion your announcement party must have been! I am very sorry that my career girl obligations kept me from coming. Martha wrote me a note, and yesterday I received the clippings you sent. Having the announcements concealed in the bouquets was a clever idea. Everyone must have been surprised, because you have made up your mind so quickly. Please convey to John my congratulations on having won the finest girl I know! May the accompanying little gift say what my adjectives cannot.

Affectionately,
Susan

Hampton Arms
March 1

184 Juneau Apartments
March 1

Dear John,

Congratulations, old man! The news of the announcement made by Joan's mother has traveled fast. You have won a beautiful and accomplished girl and one that will, I'm sure, be the best of companions.

Sincerely yours,
Kerwin Johnson

After John and Joan are engaged, the groom's mother writes to Joan.

> Château Champlain
> Quebec, Canada
> March 6

My dear Joan,

John has written us of the joy that has come into his life. We want to know you, Joan, and hope that you may be able to visit us soon. Here in Quebec March is a beautiful sunny month when the skiing is at its best. The trails at Lac Beauport offer sport for both the daring and the cautious. The rinks here in the park below our windows afford the best of skating, with good orchestras to add to the fun. Bring your snow clothes and let us have the pleasure of a visit with you the last week of March.

Mr. Lacerte is writing you a note, too.

> Most sincerely,
> Marie Lacerte

> Château Champlain
> Quebec, Canada
> March 6

My dear Joan,

John has spoken of you very often, and now his mother and I are so happy that you will become our daughter. I am looking forward to meeting you and hope you can come to visit us in March. We'll promise you outdoor sports and a hearty welcome.

> Yours sincerely,
> George Lacerte

Because Joan was still working, she was unable to accept the hospitable invitation.

> March 12

My dear Mrs. Lacerte,

Your invitation sounds so tempting, and I am so eager to meet John's parents, I just wish I could come at the end of March. Unfortunately, I have to continue my work until April thirtieth, and as my long-suffering employer has given me so many days off already, I don't dare ask for a week in March.

However, June will be here before we all know it, and then I'll have, among other happinesses, the happiness of meeting you. With all my gratitude for your lovely invitation and for your having such a wonderful son,

Yours most affectionately,
Joan

March 12

Dear Mr. Lacerte,

Your very nice note and invitation came a few days ago. I am so sorry I cannot come in March to visit you and Mrs. Lacerte, but as I explained to her, I must remain at my work. I do hope to sample some of your famous skiing and skating later on, and meanwhile I'm counting the days until June, when you both will be here for our wedding.

Yours most sincerely,
Joan

One of Joan's friends gives a linen shower for her before the wedding, using a calling card to convey the invitation:

Mrs. Jeremy Taylor
Linen Shower for Miss Joan Hobart
June 1, 3 p.m.

WEDDING

Formal Invitations

The wedding invitations may be formal, engraved folded sheets:

Mr. and Mrs. John Colan Hobart
request the honor of your presence
at the marriage of their daughter
Joan
to
Mr. John Francis Lacerte
on Saturday, the fifteenth of June
at half past three o'clock
Saint Michael's Church

or

> Mr. and Mrs. John Colan Hobart
> request the honor of
> (name written in)'s
> presence at the marriage of their daughter
> Joan
> to
> Mr. John Francis Lacerte
> on the afternoon of Saturday, the fifteenth of June
> at half past three o'clock, Saint Michael's Church
> Delevan, Wisconsin

If the church is large and many invitations have been issued, a card accompanies the invitation. On it is engraved:

> The card: *Please present this card at*
> *Saint Michael's Church*
> *on the afternoon of Saturday,*
> *June the fifteenth*

> The invitation: *Mr. and Mrs. John Colan Hobart*
> *request the honor of*
> *your presence*
> *at the marriage of their daughter*
> *Joan*
> *to*
> *Mr. John Francis Lacerte*
> *on Saturday, the fifteenth of June*
> *at three-thirty o'clock*
> *at St. Michael's Church*
> *in Delevan, Wisconsin*

The visiting cards of the bride's and groom's mothers are sometimes enclosed with the invitations for special friends whom the families want seated in the reserved section:

Bride's Section   Groom's Section
  Mrs. John Colan Hobart   *Mrs. George Lacerte*

An invitation to both the wedding and reception is engraved as follows:

> Mr. and Mrs. John Colan Hobart
> request the honor of your presence
> at the marriage of their daughter
> Joan
> to
> Mr. John Francis Lacerte
> on Saturday, the fifteenth of June
> at half past three o'clock
> at Saint Michael's Church
> and afterwards at "The Willows"
> Delevan

R.S.V.P.

A separate reception card is sent with the wedding invitation when only some of the guests are being invited to the reception or breakfast. It is about half the size of the wedding invitation and is on the same kind of paper:

> Mr. and Mrs. Graham Taylor Ross
> request the pleasure of your company
> at the wedding breakfast of their daughter
> Genevieve
> and
> Mr. Harold Ashley Mason
> on Saturday the tenth of June
> at one o'clock
> at Five hundred and twenty Harrison Avenue

R.S.V.P.

The expression, "pleasure of your company," is used instead of "honor of your presence" for breakfast and reception invitations.

Informal Invitations

For a home wedding, those invited to the wedding stay for whatever additional entertainment is given. There is then no mention made on the invitation of breakfast or reception. Sometimes there are no guests at the wedding ceremony itself and only invitations to a reception are sent. (See *Other Wedding Formalities* below.)

When a wedding is very small and no invitations are engraved, then personal notes are written to the few friends whose presence is desired.

Dear Gretchen,

Robert and I are to be married at Saint Michael's Church Monday the eighth at eight o'clock in the morning. We want you to be sure to come and to stay on afterward for a breakfast on our porch.

Affectionately,
Caroline

Other Wedding Formalities

A card engraved like the following is sometimes enclosed with an invitation to let friends know the future address of the couple. It is more usually enclosed with wedding announcements.

Mr. and Mrs. Lewis Conklin Brice
will be at home
after the first of November
at 108 Golf View Apartments
Saint Paul, Minnesota

A visiting card, with the address in the lower right corner, can be used instead.

Mr. and Mrs. Lewis Conklin Brice
108 Golf View Apartments
Saint Paul, Minnesota

If the wedding is to be a small one for only relatives and intimate friends, other acquaintances are often invited to a reception. This invitation is the same size as a wedding invitation and it is engraved:

Mr. and Mrs. Guy Brooks Hadley
request the pleasure of your company
at the wedding reception of their daughter
Stella Mary
and
Mr. William Gordon Brooks
on Wednesday, the twentieth of June
at four o'clock
Ninety-eight Garden Road

R.S.V.P.

In the case of a marriage for which a more distant relative issues the invitations:

> *Mr. and Mrs. Carl Evans Smith*
> *request the honor of your presence*
> *at the marriage of their niece*
> *Esther Marie Jones*
> *to*
> *Mr. Charles Leslie Taylor*

If "R.S.V.P." is indicated for a wedding or for a formal breakfast, luncheon, or supper, a formal reply should be written.

> Miss Elvira Stephens
> accepts with pleasure the kind invitation
> of
> Mr. and Mrs. John Colan Hobart
> for the marriage of their daughter with
> Mr. John Francis Lacerte
> Saturday, the fifteenth of June
> and to the dinner which will follow

Postponements

If a wedding has to be postponed, printed notices (if time permits) or written cards are sent to those who have received invitations. They may be worded as follows:

Owing to the illness of their daughter, Stella Mary, Mr. and Mrs. Guy Brooks Hadley announce that her marriage has been postponed.

or:

Mr. and Mrs. Guy Brooks Hadley wish to announce that the marriage of their daughter, Stella Mary, will not take place on the twentieth of June at Ninety-eight Garden Road.

Replies to Gifts

A calling card or a plain signed card accompanies the wedding gift. Letters of thanks for the gifts should follow within a few days after they have been received. As they are always sent to the bride, she acknowledges them in her own handwriting even though she may not know her husband's friends who sent them.

Dear Mrs. Culver,

    The carving set that you and Mr. Culver sent us is most handsome, and I know that when John carves my first roast with it, he will think the roast is tender! We both appreciate it so much and are looking forward to knowing you when we are in our new home in Milwaukee.

Yours sincerely,
Joan Hobart

June eighth

Dear Mr. Jacobs,

    I am really thrilled with the beautiful tea service you sent John and me. I shall be very proud to use it, and I hope you will be one of the first to come and have tea with us when we are in our new home.

Most appreciatively,
Joan Hobart

June eighth

Wedding Announcements

    Immediately after the wedding, cards of announcements are sent to those who were not invited to the wedding. The announcements may be folded sheets similar to the invitations, or they may be large engraved cards:

Mr. and Mrs. John Colan Hobart
have the honor to announce
the marriage of their daughter
Joan
to
Mr. John Francis Lacerte
on Saturday, June the fifteenth
at St. Michael's Church
Delevan, Wisconsin

    If there is no near relative to announce the marriage of an older widow, the announcement engraved on notepaper reads:

Mrs. Josephine Gates Murray
and
Mr. Theodore Coates Peak
have the honor to announce their marriage
on Wednesday, the nineteenth of June
at the Cathedral
Duluth, Minnesota

There is some precedent for the widow's use of her deceased husband's name until she remarries, even in an announcement of this type. Thus: *Mrs. Randolph Murray.*

A divorcée's announcement would read similarly except that she might use her maiden last name together with the name of her divorced husband. Therefore, Martina Blake, who has married and then divorced Mr. Francis Jones, might go by the name Mrs. Blake Jones. She could use this form in the announcement of her remarriage.

Wedding Anniversaries

For anniversaries:

Hobart-Tyler

19——   *19——*

Mr. and Mrs. John Colan Hobart
request the pleasure of your company
on Wednesday, June the twenty-sixth
from four until seven o'clock
The Willows
309 River Avenue

CALLING CARDS FOR INVITATIONS

Calling cards—which simply have one's name printed on them —are useful for inserting in gifts and flowers, as a note form for sending regrets to an invitation, or for expressing condolences or greetings to a convalescent.

After Joan has been entertained many times as a bride in Milwaukee, she begins to repay her indebtedness, using calling cards to convey invitations:

Mrs. John Lacerte
To meet Miss Emily Sears
March eighth
Tea at four

Mrs. John Lacerte
Bridge Luncheon
June twenty-sixth
One o'clock

Two or three women may join in giving a reception. In that case the names all appear on the invitation:

Mrs. Esmond Pembroke
Mrs. Carlyle Tainter
Mrs. Nelson Case Holmes
At Home
Friday afternoon, January the fifteenth,
From four till six o'clock
At The Rock River Country Club

If the reception is to be a garden party, then the words *Garden party* appear at the lower left corner of the invitation.

ADDRESSING INVITATIONS

One invitation addressed to *Mr. and Mrs. Stephen C. Blake* is sufficient for a married couple, one for sisters, addressed to *The Misses Baldwin;* but separate invitations are required for a mother and daughter, a father and son, or a brother and sister.

REPLYING TO INVITATIONS

A formal reply to a formal invitation is in good taste for an affair where one's company has been requested for a definite date.

Mr. and Mrs. Kenneth Sabin
accept with pleasure
the kind invitation of
Mr. and Mrs. Esmond Pembroke
for Thursday, January the first

A note extending an invitation should be answered by a note, but no reply is necessary when the invitation is a statement of an "At Home," unless an R.S.V.P. appears on it.

SCHOOL FUNCTIONS

At Riverview School where Ruth is a senior, festivities are in order before Christmas vacation:

The Faculty
and
The Class of Nineteen hundred and sixty-two
of Riverview School
request the pleasure of your presence
at the
Christmas Play
on Friday, the nineteenth of December
at eight o'clock
La Crosse, Wisconsin

R.S.V.P.   *Dancing ten until twelve*

The reply follows:

Mr. John Smith Kingsley
accepts with pleasure the kind invitation
of the Faculty and the Class of Nineteen hundred and
sixty-two of the Riverview School
for the Christmas play and dance
on Friday, the nineteenth of December

While Ruth was at Riverview, she heard from one of her friends at the University of Wisconsin:

Telephone
BAdger 4-6200

Pi Alpha Delta House
25 Butler Court
Madison, Wisconsin
October 26

Dear Ruth,

We Badgers have a losing team, but a winning spirit—and there's always Saturday night at the Union! November 6 is the Iowa game. Could you make it?

Tom

The Sigma Phi House
University of Minnesota

November 15

Dear Ruth,

Would it be possible for you to come up the weekend of the Minnesota-Michigan game? There are going to be several parties, and I think we could have a fine time.

Gordon

Helene at Saint Mary's in Shrub Oak was having her share of attention, too.

Alpha Tau Omega House
Ithaca, New York
January 8

Dear Helene,

Hope you haven't acquired so much Eastern sophistication you'd be bored by a freshman prom. Ours is February sixteenth and I'm looking forward to it—and to your coming.

And how about bringing a friend for a friend?

Let me know,

Keith

CHILDREN'S PARTIES

Children, too, have their party invitations and acceptances to write. A simple note written by a child is a good introduction to the customs of grown-ups.

Dear Mary,

On my birthday, the tenth of July, Mother is giving a splash party for me. I hope that you can come, at two. Bring your bathing suit.

Yours sincerely,
Helen

Such a note would be addressed "Miss Mary Slocum" for a little girl or "Master Peter Hobart" for a small boy. Older boys, seven and up, become impatient with the "Master" and are best addressed just "Peter Hobart."

Prepared illustrated invitations for children's parties with blanks for time, place, etc., are popular with most children, but they might agree to write out a note of invitation. It is helpful on any child's party invitation to specify the occasion for the party, to indicate whether presents, as well as the guest's presence, are expected!

ANNOUNCEMENT OF A BIRTH

To announce a birth, a tiny card for the baby may be fastened with a pink or blue ribbon to the parents' joint card.

> *Mr. and Mrs. John Lacerte*
> *Miss Agatha Lacerte*
> or:
> *Master Michael Lacerte*

The stationery store has delightful birth announcements with blanks for all the particulars about Baby. But most young mothers find the blanks inadequate to describe their firstborn (at least), and will write notes in praise of him to their close friends and relatives.

> Delevan Hospital
> July 6

Dear Anne,

Little Michael is one of the biggest and most precocious babies here, the doctor tells me. He's starting out to be the image of his grandpa! I can't wait to get home from this place, and as we're both doing fine, I may leave on Tuesday. John and I both hope you'll be coming through Milwaukee this summer and that you'll stop here a few days with us and our Mike.

> Love,
> Joan

A note in response to the announcement of Michael's arrival:

Dear Joan,

Steven and I were so delighted to receive the happy news of Michael's arrival. We wish him the best of futures, which seems assured with the parents he has. Our heartiest congratulations to proud father John. We are sending a tiny package with love for little Michael.

Affectionately,
Mary

Telegrams may be in order as quick birth announcements. They should be answered with a short note:

MISS MOWBRAY

MICHAEL ARRIVED THIS MORNING. EIGHT POUNDS. JOAN, SON DOING WELL.

In response:

MASTER MICHAEL LACERTE,

GREETINGS MY BOY. CONGRATULATIONS PROUD MOTHER AND DAD.

ELLEN MOWBRAY

THE CHRISTENING

Joan's little son is to make his first public appearance at his christening. Joan wants Mary, a childhood friend, and Louis, a young cousin of John's, to be the godparents.

Dear Mary,

Little Michael is to be baptized the first Sunday in August, at St. Bartholomew's Church, at twelve-thirty. You and I were confirmed together, so I think it will be perfect if you will be the godmother. Louis Lacerte, a cousin of John's, will be godfather. We plan to have a small luncheon at our house after the service at the church.

Mother and Dad are driving in for the service and will phone you to ask you to come with them.

Affectionately,
Joan

Dear Joan,

How can I tell you how honored I feel that you want me to be little Michael's godmother? I shall be only too proud and happy to do so. Your mother called shortly after your note came, and we are going to drive in together.

Fondly,
Mary

To acknowledge a gift from the godfather-to-be, Louis, the cousin of the baby's daddy:

Dear Louis,

The silver place setting with Michael's name on it is so beautiful, and will be a treasure to him all his life. You were so thoughtful to give him such a practical gift. The way he's growing, he'll be sitting at the table with us soon and eating with it! John is so pleased with it, too. We all send you our loving appreciation.

Devotedly yours,
Joan

Chapter Fourteen

NOTES AND REPLIES

NOTES OF CONGRATULATION

The pleasure of a success is always heightened by a note of congratulation from a friend:

> The Willows
> 309 River Avenue
> June 20

Dear Miss Cooper,

Many times when Ruth and Joan were in your class I wanted to write to tell you how fine a teacher I thought they had. When I read in the *Gazette* this evening that you have been appointed Principal of the Lincoln School, I just had to comment on what a perfect choice has been made. May you be very happy in your new position. I know that all who work with you will be!

> Yours most sincerely,
> Janet Hobart

> The Willows
> Delevan, Wisconsin
> January 15

My dear Carl,

Heartiest congratulations on your election to the office of president of the State Medical Association. Your colleagues have made a wise choice, for if ever there was man with the interests of his profession at heart, it is you. May you have a free hand to accomplish your plans and to use some of your excellent ideas.

> Faithfully yours,
> John Hobart

December 3

Dear Harold,

John and I heard through the grapevine last evening that you are to be the new manager of Thomas and Silby. You have given them so many years of devoted, intelligent service that you have certainly deserved this. Our congratulations to you and to T. and S. also for having chosen the right man!

May all go beautifully in the new position. Say hello to Harriet for me.

Cordially,
Janet Hobart

A Delevan friend of Ruth's wins out in a swimming meet:

Riverview School
November 6

Dear Jerry,

Mother sent me the clippings about your success at the swimming meet. Naturally, I am not surprised at all, but I thought I'd just say "Congratulations." Where are you going to find room for another silver cup?

Some of our girls may be going up to the Tri-State meet, if the red tape unrolls straight, and there I shall expect to see you win again.

When we're all home for Thanksgiving vacation we'll have to hold a real celebration.

Your one-time swimming rival,
Ruth

An awkward situation, such as the following one, can be graciously explained in a note. Lennie Kingston was playing in a tennis match at Waukesha. She had come onto the court wearing her wrist watch. As she changed courts, she quickly handed it to a girl watching the line fouls, Jane Tasman. Jane left with the watch after the match, neither girl having remembered it in the excitement at the end of the tournament.

1128 Juneau Parkway
Milwaukee 14, Wisconsin
August 18

My dear Miss Kingston,

Imagine my embarrassment when I was taking a handkerchief from my purse last night to find your watch there! In the midst of the excitement at the end of the match, and in my hurry to get to my car and back to Milwaukee for an appointment, I never once thought of your watch. I hope missing it did not alarm you, and that you could remember to whom you hurriedly handed it. I have mailed it to you by insured parcel post and shall keep the receipt until I hear from you that you have received it safe and sound.

Now that the watch is off my mind, I can congratulate you on your splendid performance yesterday afternoon. It takes a cool head to come from behind like that and ward off two set, match, and championship points. I hope that next year you will enter bigger and better tournaments. I am sure you would shine again in them.

> With best wishes for your future success,
> Jane Tasman

Naturally, Lennie Kingston wrote immediately to Miss Tasman to assure her the watch was in good condition. She enclosed postage to cover the cost of mailing it.

807 Tenth Avenue
Waukesha, Wisconsin
August 19

My dear Miss Tasman,

Thank you so much for taking care of my watch for me and then for your kindness in mailing it to me. I was conscious of it on my wrist when serving, so I took it off and give it to the first person I saw. I am glad it fell into such careful hands. Thank you, too, for your compliments and kind wishes. I think maybe my opponent was a little upset by the ball she put outside at the critical moment, for the breaks came my way after that.

> Most sincerely yours,
> Lennie Kingston

The names of the boys receiving letters for service on the Delevan school football team of 1961 were published in *The*

Janeston News. As the schools of the two towns had been rivals for years, the players knew each other rather well. One of the Janeston boys wrote to congratulate a friendly rival:

1295 Main Street
Janeston, Wisconsin
January 31

Dear Buck,

In last night's paper, I read that your football coach had presented letters to the squad. Congratulations! You must be mighty proud to have three D's for football. Most fellows have to be content to get one. Funny how sentimental people get over letters they win for sports. Dad was showing me his high school and college letters the other day. He says he treasures them among his choicest possessions. I noticed he didn't have to go very far down in the old trunk to get them. I suppose we'll be showing ours to some sons some day!

Your old opposition,
Dick

Obtaining an advanced degree is a great event in the life of professional people. Congratulations are in order for a successful student:

My dear Norma,

To think that you have now satisfied a lifelong ambition and can write Ph.D. after your name! My heartiest congratulations! It has been interesting work every hour of each day, I know, and receiving the degree shows how you have concentrated during those hours. It takes not only ability, but physical fitness, for it must be a great strain. I am so happy you have been able to see it through.

Your plans for a summer at the lake where you can swim, fish, sleep, and hike with lots of fresh air to breathe sound just right. It also sounds as though you have planned a sensible balance of solitude and guests! You will emerge with new vitality for classes in October, I am sure. After the year's leave of absence, you must be anxious to return to your beloved campus.

With best wishes for every future success, and with keen anticipation of seeing you in a few weeks,

Most affectionately,
Agnes

June 30

While those who have succeeded enjoy receiving letters of congratulations, it is those who have had a failure who *need* an encouraging note from a friend—a slightly more difficult note to write!

> The Willows
> 309 River Avenue
> Delevan, Wisconsin
> June 10

Dearest Esther,

Marion Strong wrote me that you were back at home and quite upset that the secretarial position had not turned out well. From what she said, you must have been given an inaccurate picture of what was expected of you. I have heard of many similar cases, and knowing you, I know how much you have to offer in work truly fitted to you.

Now, I have a favor to ask of you. John takes off for Chicago June 26 for two weeks. Could you come here then for a couple of weeks and keep me company? We could have a really relaxed time, go on a few little sprees hereabouts, dip in the lake, and have some picnics. I would just love to have you here.

I wanted to ask you to think this over, too; John has a friend over in Janeston who needs a secretary in September. He wants a mature, dependable person, and he does *not* require a knowledge of any specialized vocabularies! We mentioned you to him, and he would like to talk to you. If you would be interested, I'll tell you all the details when you get here. There's no hurry about it yet, as he has temporary help until September, so we can enjoy our visit first.

Do say you can come to see me. Our garden will be looking pretty for you about then, and we can promise you some strawberries.

> Love,
> Janet

ASKING FAVORS

To ask a favor, to express thanks, sympathy or congratulation, a note with no extraneous details is always adequate. One may use the folded note sheet, a small informal, a single sheet with the monogram or address, or a plain sheet. Mr. Hobart writes to a vacationing friend asking to borrow a portable radio:

February 16

Dear Dave,

It's good the storm here held off for your flight, and by now you and Sue must have your first Florida sunburn! To make you enjoy yourselves more, the weather here has been terrible.

When you left us your key for emergencies, I didn't think that I'd be taking advantage of you. However, I have a favor to ask.

That little cold Janet had grew into a bad cough, and Dr. Farley told her she has to stay in bed for a while. Ruth has our small radio in Riverview and you know how Janet is about the news.

I was wondering whether I could borrow your portable radio from the recreation room until she comes downstairs. This might keep her up there a little longer. I'd appreciate it very much, Dave.

I've looked in on your house several times and everything is fine. Have a great time!

Sincerely,
John

Dave replies by special delivery from Florida:

February 19

Dear John,

Take the radio, of course. You should have taken it immediately. The television in the rec room is easy to lift off its table, and Janet might like that to vary things a little. Sue and I are so sorry she's ill and hope that she recovers rapidly. We wish she and you could share some of this sunny weather with us.

Thanks for watching the house. And take good care of your patient!

As ever,
Dave

GIFT NOTES

A gift came from Joyce Ralston to Agnes Farnsworth, a teacher at Riverview School. The card accompanying it read:

from Joyce
With love and congratulations

The reply:

Dear Joyce,

The box of chocolates came by the morning delivery on my birthday. You must have remembered my special love for Maude Brown's chocolates. I was delighted to have some to share with friends who came to play bridge that evening.

I can't tell you how nice it was to have you remember my birthday, and in such a pleasant way.

I'm leaving on my vacation Wednesday, and then I'll write you all the accumulated news.

Yours gratefully,
Agnes

After many years of service at Riverview School, Miss Swift, one of the Latin instructors, has decided to leave. Her classes present her with a parting gift.

RIVERVIEW SCHOOL
LA CROSSE, WISCONSIN

May 30

Dear Miss Swift,

It is hard to tell you how sorry we are that you are leaving Riverview. The girls who have completed their academic work with you have been so fortunate. The rest of us can only hope that we shall prove a credit to your training. We all want to express our appreciation of your interest in us and to thank you for the happy hours we have spent in your classes.

We hope the traveling case will be useful to you on your trip this summer and a constant reminder of the love and devotion of your students. The classes have paid me the compliment of asking me to write you this note.

Most sincerely yours,
Elizabeth Bryant

A reply to a gift of flowers sent while Ruth Hobart was in the hospital:

Dear George,

Thank you so much for the gorgeous chrysanthemums. They almost compensated for my not being able to make it to your party last

Saturday. I may have my first visitors tomorrow between four and five, and, if you have nothing important to do, I'd love to see you.

Sincerely,
Ruth

Dear Mrs. Reynolds,

The African violet you sent me is right near me on my bedside table. One of the blossoms opened just this morning. You were so very thoughtful to send it. I am going to take it back to Riverview to have in my bay window all winter, and I hope when I'm back, you will come up to see it, and me!

Affectionately,
Ruth Hobart

SCHOOL EXCUSES

Notes must often be written to excuse a child's absence at school or to ask some favor of the authorities. Such a note should be written on note paper and enclosed in an envelope which is not to be sealed.

My dear Miss Farnham,

Will you kindly excuse John's absence on Monday and Tuesday? Mr. Kent took him to Chicago to consult an oculist.

Very truly yours,
Mary Tate Kent
(Mrs. E. B. Kent)

25 Mill Lane
March 15

Misunderstandings sometimes arise between school and home. Notes from Mother should not be written in anger, but with consideration for the many kinds of pressure teachers have to bear:

March 13

Dear Mr. Torrence,

I am anxious to clarify the situation which ended with Ken's being sent to the office yesterday. He really was telling the truth when he insisted he was not supposed to take gym. Of course, I know he does try to get out of games because of his poor vision, but yesterday I had written a note asking that you excuse him from gym and the shower because he had had a sore throat all weekend. He must have dropped the note on the street when he reached for his school bus ticket. He was quite upset about being sent to the office, and I am sure all this was none too pleasant for you either. I am also writing Miss Cooper an explanation.

We have sent away for a glasses' shield for him, and when he can wear that in gym class he may be less reluctant to play the games.

I hope to be able to talk to you at school soon to see what else you think we could do here at home to encourage Ken.

> Yours sincerely,
> Gertrude Walsh
> (Mrs. Robert Walsh)

NOTES OF APOLOGY TO NEIGHBORS

A note to a neighbor is often necessary and more gracious than a phone call, especially when the neighbor is not an intimate acquaintance. It can help by giving the neighbor time to consider a reply.

My dear Mrs. Weld,

Unfortunately, our dog Scotty has been scratching in your garden and has ruined your pretty pansies. I am so sorry. We have asked the Wolfe Greenhouse to supply you with new plants, and they will be phoning to take your order tomorrow. We have long talked of enclosing our lawn with a fence, and at last we have that ordered, too! Meanwhile, I'll keep Scotty tied up and see that he buries his bones in his own yard.

> Sincerely yours,
> Joan Lacerte

My dear Mrs. Kenyon,

I find that Michael has broken a window in your basement. Maybe all little boys have to find out that balls can break glass, but I am sorry it was your window and not ours that he used for his experiment. Max

Schliemann, phone RI 9-3232, does repairing for us. If you will let him know when it would be convenient for you to have a new pane put in, he will replace the glass and charge the amount to us.

> Very truly yours,
> Joan Lacerte
> (Mrs. J. F. Lacerte)

Monday

BROKEN APPOINTMENTS

My dear Ann,

I am just terribly sorry I couldn't get to the club this afternoon. I would have called you, but I was hunting frantically for little Michael for almost two hours. He was out in the yard at noon and just vanished. Mrs. Bannister, our sitter, and I combed the neighborhood calling him and getting more and more frightened.

When I decided to go home and call the police, didn't I find my precious sound asleep on his blanket in his *closet!* Of course, then, he woke up hungry and furious, and it was too late for club.

Please forgive us, Ann, and come here next week, for I believe it's my turn to entertain.

> Most contritely,
> Joan

Friday evening

ILLNESS NOTES

When Peter Hobart was ill, his teacher wrote a note:

> Room 107
> The Lincoln School
> February 8

Dear Peter,

The school nurse tells me you have the measles and must be absent for three weeks. There are several others in the same condition. Do be careful while you are ill to protect your eyes. Don't think of doing any reading. We'll have reviews when the measley ones all return. Since you are not to watch television either, perhaps you can listen to radio programs to help pass the time while you recuperate. I asked Bud to bring you one of my albums of "I Can Speak French" records, as he said you have a player at home. I think you might find them fun. We all miss you and shall be happy when you return.

Sincerely yours,
Marjorie Tenant

His neighbor pal sends over a note:

Dear Peter,

Mom says you have measles, but aren't very sick. I can't come over to play with you, and you can't come out. I'll bring my feeding station and put it up in the tree where you can see it from bed. Maybe my cardinals will come along. Watch their tails when they spread. The female does a lot more hopping around and comes oftener, but the male is prettier. I'll bet you can't tell the color of the bill of each by tomorrow at ten A.M. Feed them morning glory seeds and cracked corn. They won't eat suet.

I have just finished reading *Tom Sawyer*. Get your mother to read it aloud to you. It's a good story.

Bud

Peter greatly appreciated the feeding station put up for him by his pal. His period of quarantine passed more rapidly, watching for the birds each day. Naturally, after his recovery, he wanted to do something for Bud. Mr. Hobart's offer to take the boys to Madison for the basketball tournament met with Peter's instant approval. He sat down at once to write a short note to Bud.

Dear Bud,

Dad says he will take you and me to Madison on Saturday to see Delevan play Cambridge in the afternoon, if you can go. I hope your dad will let you. We are to start about a quarter to eleven, have lunch at the Royce Homestead, see the game, and maybe take a look in the capitol building. Then we'll stop again with Mrs. Royce to have baked ham and sweet potatoes for dinner. I'm going light on food from now till Saturday to have plenty of room. It will all be great if you can go, too. Delevan 20—Cambridge 18?

Your friend,
Peter

Wednesday

A letter to a teacher after special assistance has been given to Ruth:

The Willows
Delevan, Wisconsin
November 20

My dear Miss Swift,

Ruth's letter today has informed her father and me how kind you have been to her, and how you have helped her to cover the week's translation she missed while in the hospital. Your interest will certainly be reflected in her attitude toward her work.

If Ruth needs more help, will you have time to give her regular tutoring for a few lessons? When I left she was making such good progress that I think she will be back on regular schedule very shortly.

Mr. Hobart joins me in wishing you a happy and successful school year.

Most sincerely yours,
Janet Hobart
(Mrs. J. C. Hobart)

To a hospitalized friend at Christmas, Mrs. Hobart writes:

Dear Mrs. Bennett,

Today when I was selecting Christmas cards for my cousin who is ill, I saw these with the little lambs and I couldn't resist getting some for you, thinking of the days we fed your little lamb from the bottle. I hope you can accommodate these few extra ones.

I am glad to hear from Mr. Bennett that the hospital chart is registering your steady improvement. You will be pleased to know that when I dropped in at your home yesterday, the most savory whiffs from newly baked pie emerged! Angie has turned out to be a fine cook. Your family is managing really well. My husband and I both wish you a speedy recovery.

Most sincerely yours,
Janet Hobart

CONDOLENCES

Letters of condolence are generally brief and do not enlarge in detail on the good qualities of the deceased. Such letters are written with the idea of helping the bereaved to live through trying days and not reminding them of a loss they feel very keenly.

A brief note of sympathy:

My dear Susan,
　　Please accept my sincere sympathy for you in your sorrow.

Fondly,
Mary Walter

315 South Sixth Street
Tuesday

A visiting card, a folder, or a plain card is sent with flowers:

Miss Maureen Scranton
With love and deepest sympathy

A longer note of sympathy:

Dear Susan,
　　The news of your sorrow has just reached me. I think I can realize your loss because I know how empty my world seemed when I heard of the passing of your mother. It will be very hard for all of us who knew her well to carry on without her, but we can be glad it was our privilege to have come in contact as long as we did with such a very lovely person. I shall always remember her kindness and cleverness.

Very sincerely,
Martha

Riverview School
Wednesday

Replies may be written any time within six weeks after the arrival of the notes or flowers, or intimate relatives may write the letters acknowledging their receipt.

My dear Mr. Wyckham,
　　Thank you for the flowers and for the expression of sympathy. Your words of comfort were most helpful.

Most sincerely yours,
Thelma C. Grant

My dear Martha,

Your letter and flowers reached me Thursday. Thank you so much for your thoughts. I shall try to return to school on Tuesday. Will you convey my thanks and appreciation to all the girls who wrote to me so kindly?

Lovingly,
Susan

ASKING SOMEONE TO APPEAR ON A PROGRAM

From a near-by town a letter comes to Mrs. Hobart requesting assistance on a club program:

318 Doswell Avenue
Fort Atkinson, Wisconsin
December 8

My dear Mrs. Hobart,

The Travel Group of our Women's Club plans to devote a meeting to Williamsburg, and we should like to have you give the program with those wonderful slides you showed at the Palmers' last month. This meeting will be on Tuesday, February 18, and you could make the same kind of informal commentary you did at the Palmers' with perhaps a few additional remarks about routes to Williamsburg and accommodations. A half hour with a question period of fifteen minutes is the usual length of our programs.

The Travel Group wants you as its luncheon guest beforehand. I would plan to meet you in front of the Women's Club here at 12:15 and provide helping hands to bring in your slides. The club projector and screen will be available.

We all do hope you can come and give us your colorful and informative travelogue.

Very sincerely yours,
Ann Green Cole

My dear Mrs. Tennant,

Some unexpected changes at our home will make it impossible for me to take my part on the program for the Women's Club this winter. I am very sorry as I am decidedly interested in the topic assigned to me and should have enjoyed doing the necessary reading. I hesitated to ask anyone to take my place before informing you as you may have someone in mind; but if you haven't, I think Mrs. Wallace may be willing. She has a cousin who has been in Lima on business and has therefore close access to material on Peru.

Believe me, it is with real regret that I must give up active club participation.

Yours very truly,
Eleanor Carey

64 Wentworth Avenue
November 2

May 14

My dear Mrs. Hobart,

Ruth has often told me of your visit to Williamsburg, Virginia, and of the pictures that you brought home with you. In American History class, we have been talking about the restorations there. Would you be willing to come to school some day next week to tell us about your trip and show us some of your slides? Our classes are forty minutes long.

Yours truly,
Cora Strong

May 18

My dear Cora,

Your request to bring my slides and speak to the American History class finds me in the midst of a busy week, but it is hard to refuse students when they are in earnest over some project. So you may count on me Friday at two o'clock for forty minutes. I'll bring some cards and snapshots of Williamsburg to pass around the class and also a few other souvenirs that you might find amusing.

The school projector shows my slides satisfactorily; I used it at a P.T.A. meeting last autumn. I am in no sense a lecturer, but if my pictures and descriptions will add to the pleasure of your study, I shall be delighted. I do hope some of you will become interested in going there when you are older, as Williamsburg inspires a deep respect for our American heritage.

Affectionately yours,
Janet Hobart
(Mrs. J. C. Hobart)

Thank you notes for gifts and for favors can be lengthy or brief, but they always mention the kindness and add a thought or two about how much it is appreciated. It is possible to buy cards printed with "Thank You" to acknowledge an attention, but to send such a card with a signature only is not making gratitude as evident as it might be.

Dear Mrs. Hobart,

Our American History class was delighted and inspired by your talk yesterday. You had to leave so quickly, all we could do to show you our appreciation was to applaud. We hope you will enjoy the lilies of the valley a fraction as much as we did the pictures.

Most sincerely yours,
Cora Strong

May 22

NOTES OF INTRODUCTION

If we are positive a friend traveling or moving would be congenial with friends who live where he is going, we can write a note of introduction to those in the new locality. In almost all circumstances it is best to leave the initiative there, rather than causing unwanted obligations by sending the newcomer directly to them. Joan Lacerte writes to introduce some vacationing friends:

June 21

Dear Dot,

While you and Dick don't exactly lack company at Eager Beaver Lodge, you might enjoy meeting a couple we know who will be vacationing at Totem Inn across the bay, July 2 through 16. They are Jill and Tommy Fabien. Tommy works with John. He and Jill have been married just one year. They both love fishing, even as much as you two, and I'm sure they'd relish some of Dick's fish stories.

So if you can find time to activate the putt-putt and go visit them, they'd probably be delighted.

Little Michael says "Hi!" to your future Miss Universe. When and if he takes a nap some day, I'll write you all the gossip.

Love,
Joan

Dot replies from her cottage:

June 24

Dear Joan,

We were so glad to hear about your friends coming to Totem Inn and have left a message there for them to call us when they get settled. Life has been a little too quiet at Eager Beaver. Betty couldn't come at the last minute, having sprained her ankle, and Miss Universe is spending two weeks with Dick's family. The Campbells next to us won't be up until August, and an older couple is renting the Walden's cottage.

We have just discovered a bay where there are too many bass, even for us, and we plan to let the Fabiens in on it!

More later,
Love,
Dot

Recommendation to a Sorority

Joan has met a girl who she believes would enjoy sorority life at the university and who would have much to contribute to a group that will pledge her.

The Willows
Delevan, Wisconsin
August 16

Dear Muriel,

While visiting my mother, I met a very likeable girl who expects to enter the University of Wisconsin in September. Knowing that you are always glad to hear of new girls at rushing time, I am sure you will want to add the name of Judy Milnes to your list. She is the daughter of the new rector at Saint Michael's in Delevan, has lived most of her life in Ontario, California, but finished her senior year at Riverview School in La Crosse. She is excellent at tennis. Because I feel sure the Alpha Beta girls will find her congenial, I have invited her to drive to Milwaukee with Ruth and me and hope that you and Katy will have luncheon with us next Tuesday at one o'clock.

Please give my fond regards to your mother.

Affectionately,
Joan

After Muriel and Katy had met Judy, they notified their rushing chairman at the university about the prospective freshman. Joan soon received a note of thanks for having recommended a new girl:

Wisconsin Beta of Alpha Beta Sigma appreciates your recommendation of Judy Milnes and will extend all courtesy and consideration.

> Grace Grayman
> Rushing Chairman

INVITATIONS TO VISIT

For a Short Visit

One may want to send an informal note to a good friend to visit at a summer cottage:

Dearest Paula,

Here Michael and I are, comfortably settled in a roomy cottage on the shore of Mishewawa. John drives out each night—only twenty miles from the office. Can't you and Robin join us for a couple of weeks? We would so love to have you. We have fresh vegetables and milk each day from the Hazelnut Farms. The swimming is good. Bob and John can arrange to go back and forth together.

> Fondly yours,
> Joan

Box 64
Rural Route 3
Waukesha

Of course Paula is delighted to accept:

Dear Joan,

Thank you a thousand times for your invitation. Bob will drive us out Thursday. I'll have the car packed full in the morning and then Bob and John can stop for Robin and me at five. I'll have a chicken and dessert ready, so you count on preparing just vegetables that night. Am checking off the minutes until I see you.

> Lovingly,
> Paula

Tuesday

A few days after her return to Milwaukee, Paula wrote Joan a note to thank her for her hospitality. (See *Bread-and-Butter Letters*.)

The Week-End and House Party

The week-end or house party is an informal gathering to which guests are invited by notes. The length of the visit is indicated, and arrangements are made for meeting guests at the station if they are not driving. Train schedules can be enclosed.

An informal verbal invitation, issued some months ahead when friends are together, should be repeated by a written note as the time for the house party approaches—in plenty of time to allow the guests to fit the week-end into their schedules.

Dear George,

We are inviting five of Ruth's friends to spend the week-end with us at The Willows, July 14–17. Will you join us? There will be a dance at the Lake Ripley Country Club, a barbecue at our home, golf, the annual yacht races at Delevan Lake, and as much tennis as you like.

We shall hope to see you Friday, the 14th, about four o'clock.

Most sincerely yours,
Janet Hobart

Delevan
July 1

16 Crowell Place
La Crosse, Wisconsin
July 3

Dear Mrs. Hobart,

I shall be very happy to accept your kind invitation for the weekend of the 14th. I shall drive over on Friday, reaching "The Willows" in the late afternoon, barring traffic jams. We have been playing much tennis here this summer, and I'm looking forward to some doubles on your court.

My best regards to you and Ruth.

Most sincerely yours,
George Cass

Mutual friends of Mr. and Mrs. Hobart are going to meet in Ontario, Canada:

>   Arrowhead Lake
>   Woodville, Ontario
>   July 30

Dear Margaret,

You mentioned you were driving up through Algonquin Park in August, and you mustn't pass so nearby without a visit at Arrowhead Lake. Could you come Friday, August 8th through the 11th? There would be much doing for Bob and Peggy over the weekend, including a square dance in Woodville Saturday night. Tell Bob we now have water skis—and plenty of volunteers to man the outboard.

David has found a trail leading to a waterfall that Jack might like to photograph. The blueberries will be in their prime then, too!

It should take you about an hour to drive in here from Emerald Lake. The road is much better than it was last summer. We'll expect you about 4:30 Friday, the 8th, in time for a swim!

>   Fondly,
>   Patricia

A written invitation to a house party requires an immediate answer containing explicit information about arrival:

Dear Patricia,

Your invitation was most welcome. Jack and I shall be delighted to spend the 8th through the 11th week-end with you at Arrowhead. Bob and Peggy have voted that the high point of our trip, too! When we visited you last year, they had such a glorious time with all the young people at Arrowhead.

We shall take the Emerald Lake route in and should arrive just about 4:30. It will be wonderful to see you and David, go on that waterfall hike, and have some good talks around your fireplace.

>   Most affectionately,
>   Margaret

One of the Riverview faculty decided to go to Columbia University to work for her doctor's degree. She wants a friend to visit her over a weekend during the Christmas recess.

The Cathedral Residence Club
Morningside Drive
New York City
December 4

My dear Katherine,

We are having a celebration the last weekend of the year, and I am taking a little respite from my reading at the library. My dissertation is progressing as rapidly as can be expected, thank you, and will be so much the better when I view it from a new angle on Tuesday.

Can you make your promised visit to New York at Christmas time? We have tickets for *Aida*. There is a dance at the Club Saturday night to which a fellow student would like to take you. Knowing your love for music, I have accepted invitations for the Philharmonic on Sunday. You will want to hear the boy soprano at Grace Church Sunday morning. You can sleep when you return. That leaves Monday for the shops!

In expectation of seeing you step from the 2:10 train at Grand Central, Friday afternoon, the twenty-sixth,

Yours as ever,
Norma

Dear Norma,

Your letter repeating your tempting invitation has speeded up my heartbeat! at the prospect of all the fun. I shall plan to arrive on the 2:10 train at Grand Central.

I must tell you how happy I am that you have included *Aida* in our round of events. I always follow the librettos for the broadcasts with one of my friends. Now we can compare notes on the advantages of live opera versus the radio. Maybe the future Ph.D. will welcome a vacation from the library, too.

Excitedly,
Katherine

East Aurora
December 20th

Box 85
Seaside
May 19

My dear Ruth,

My mother tells me you are coming to the Pacific coast this summer to visit your cousins in California. I suppose you will be coming
by the Canadian Pacific and down the coast in order to see as much
of this Western world as you can. Mother and I want you to come
to us at Seaside for a week.

Daddy will meet your train in Portland and drive you here if you
arrive on a Saturday morning. Then you can stay here for eight days
for a good break in your trip, and Daddy will put you back on a Monday train bound for California.

Have you ever dug for clams or raked crabs from the holes in the
sand when the tide goes out? We can have beach parties and swim
in the pool. The ocean is too cold for swimming in this section. Mother
is enclosing necessary train schedules in her letter to your mother. I
do hope you can come. We can exchange all sorts of stories about
school, too.

Yours affectionately,
Ann

May 25

Dear Ann,

The visit you suggest during my trip sounds very exciting, and I
should just love to come. Mother and Dad have been studying time-
tables and maps. They had thought a little of having me fly out, but
it just happens that friends of ours are making a western trip and going
to Seattle by the Canadian Pacific; and they offered to have me join
them. We shall stop at Lake Louise on the way. Later they will put
me aboard a train for Portland, and I can visit you while they see Seattle. Mother is writing all the particulars.

I am checking off weeks and days until the great moment arrives.
I shall have material for English themes for all next winter. I'm sure
I'll be the only one in my class to have dug for clams! Mother is writ-

ing about your family's driving down to Los Angeles to meet us later in the summer when they come out to get me. Let's hope that happens too.

>With keen anticipation and love,
>Ruth

Bread-and-Butter Letters

After these gay occasions are matters of the past, but not of history, "bread-and-butter" or "thank you" letters must come quite quickly, within a week or ten days.

Dear Patricia,

The children, Jack, and I will be talking about our weekend with you for months to come. We enjoyed every minute—the deer by the waterfall, the marvelous blueberries and cream, Bob and Peggy at the square dance, and your friends the O'Briens. We especially enjoyed being with you!

Our drive home taking the Park route was very interesting—especially feeding the almost-tame deer which ate cookies from our hands! Tuesday evening we saw a bear by the road.

We hope you will plan to go home by way of Detroit so you can stay with us a night or so, although we can't promise any deer!

Jack will send the snapshots soon.

>Lovingly,
>Margaret

>July 19

Dear Mrs. Hobart,

Last weekend at your house seems a long way off already, as I am back at my job at the swimming pool! I certainly enjoyed the tennis. The yacht races—especially the upset and rescue—were great! A small box should arrive soon—just a little something to remember me by in your busy household.

>Most appreciatively yours,
>George Cass

25 Longview Terrace
Newport
June 20

My dear Dorothy,

Thank you so much for a lovely weekend. I enjoyed myself immensely, and feel very much rested and refreshed. Everything was perfect, and you are a wonderful hostess.

My love to you and Jack,
Anne

Dear Joan,

It scarcely seems possible that we are now waking up in a warm Milwaukee apartment instead of on a screened porch by the side of a lake. Those two weeks were perfect! Robin gained so much and we're all brown and summery looking now, in good shape to meet my mother in Rhinelander.

Bob and I found a wonderful picnic spot yesterday. When you come back to town in September we'll plan to take you there.

With best wishes and many thanks from all of us to all the Lacertes,

Paula

Chapter Fifteen

OTHER SOCIAL LETTERS

TRAVEL

Letters from friends on a trip should convey the joy the writer finds in seeing new sights and making new acquaintances. Such letters often sound as though written in a hurry, as most sightseers go breezing along without too much time to catch their breath.

> 17 Reed Crossing
> White Plains, New York
> April 12

Dear Ruth,

Phyllis' family is still asleep, so I'll write you until someone stirs. I'm too excited to sleep any more!

Yesterday Mr. Parker drove us in to Manhattan. At the risk of seeming like a hick I gaped out the car window at the skyline, which is too beautiful to describe. Before we parked he drove us down the West Side Highway, and we passed several huge ocean liners at the piers. Then we came up the East Side Drive to see the United Nations building, which was shining all over in the sunlight.

Thank goodness I didn't wear heels! We pushed through crowds to Fifth Avenue, where there are the most gorgeous clothes and jewelry in the elegant shop windows—and it was all out for Easter! On the street you hear every language, including Brooklynese. I saw a handsome man in a turban and a woman with green hair. Everyone rushed, pedestrians ignored red lights, and Phyllis laughed because I started rushing, too!

We shopped some. There are gifts from all over the world. It's lucky I left some money back at the Parkers! We lunched at a cozy French restaurant run by a French father, mother, and son. What manners and accents! Phyllis ordered and *ate*—ugh, snails! I had some kind of divine seafood with a cheese sauce that never came from Wisconsin.

Phyllis insisted we ride in the subway. We took an express, and the thing roared, shuddered and swerved at eighty miles an hour, it seemed. I was terrified. It was packed with people, all reading newspapers.

We did only part of the Metropolitan Museum of Art. You feel almost reverent looking at the originals of the old masters. The museum is vast; you could spend months there. Mr. Parker met us there, and drove us back to White Plains in a mad traffic jam—the after-work rush, he said.

I smell bacon, so I must hurry. Today we see a matinee of the new Tennessee Williams play. We are going with Andrew Kent, Phyllis' latest, and her brother, Jack. Jack is handsome, is taking courses in electronics, and is a tease. He said he expected me to have blonde pigtails and round, red cheeks. We'll all have supper in Greenwich Village in some arty restaurant. Sunday, there's the Easter Parade! I smell coffee, so I'll write more later.

Love,
Helene

Bon Voyage

Sailing off on a ship is probably the most thrilling beginning of any trip. The setting can't help but be exciting. The stewards, the loading of baggage, the long dock, the graceful ship, the gangplank, the shining deck and cozy cabins, the variety of strangers most of whom will be at least speaking acquaintances by the end of a week—all set one's blood a tingle, to say nothing of the anticipation of new adventures in foreign lands. Here are some notes that might be sent from the ship or dispatched by the pilot from the arrival port.

Mrs. Hobart and Joan sailed from Montreal one June. On this trip Joan was to meet her future husband. Many gifts, expressions of good will for a "bon voyage," were awaiting Joan and her mother in their cabin. Books, flowers, a basket of fruit, each bearing a card with a short inscription:

Best wishes for a good voyage
With the compliments and good wishes of —
With love and best wishes for a "bon voyage"

As soon as they could, they found the writing salon to pen a few notes of thanks to be taken by the pilot's boat at Quebec.

June 10

Dear Dad,

The flowers are beautiful! Mother and I will enjoy them at our table for several days, I know. Everything is so new and so exciting. I heard several French Canadians singing their songs as they stood on the stern waving to some friends on the dock. It is like a foreign land already. I'm all anticipation for the summer to come. I only wish you could be with us.

Love, and thank you for the wonderful trip and for the flowers.

Joan

June 10

My dear Philip,

The roses are beautiful. I have one in my hair now. The others will brighten our table and maybe our spirits if the boat begins to rock! I'm sure this is to be a wonderful summer with so wonderful a beginning.

Most sincerely,
Joan

A few people from Quebec had come to the ship to say goodbys. Brief notes, sent from Liverpool, are happily read by these friends:

June 17

Dear Monique,

How kind it was of you to come aboard at Quebec to wish us "bon voyage." It is too bad you couldn't have made the trip with us. We've had very good weather and scarcely anyone has missed meals. We've had movies, a concert by all the talented people, deck tennis and golf, a fancy dress party, countless card games, and some French every afternoon.

Your friend John, as he is known among the English people on board, has a good baritone voice. He has sung "Alouette," "A la Claire

Fontaine," and "Il était un Petit Navire" on all occasions and at the concert had everyone in the salon joining with him.

Last night we stood in the point of the prow to watch the ship's progress among the islands. The lights from the buoys flashed on and off as our course took us to the north of Ireland. This noon we sailed up the Mercy to disembark at Liverpool. Such commotion among stewards to get us to "paste our labels," have passports ready, line up for the immigration inspector, etc., etc.

I shall hope to find a letter from you somewhere in Europe. You have my itinerary.

Affectionately,
Joan

After a trip conducted by a travel bureau, previous strangers often become very good friends. Those who have taken pictures along the way may want to exchange with others who have had success with snapshots. After her trip west, Ruth found she had some very clear views taken at Lake Louise and at Glacier. She sent some prints to a woman who had a berth across the aisle.

September 4

Dear Mrs. Manson,

Did you have a wonderful summer? I hope so. Looking over my snapshots brings back many of the high spots of the summer. One of the best was the trip through the Canadian Rockies. Here are a few of my favorites.

Sincerely yours,
Ruth Hobart

HOUSEHOLD AFFAIRS

Letters written to settle household affairs and letters between members of a family are important factors in one's daily life.

A letter of reference for a servant leaving the household mentions only her good points. The omissions may be obvious to the next employer, who can always phone or write for more details. It is better to use no salutation than to write the letter "To Whom It May Concern." The writer's address appears on the letter as usual, either printed on the stationery, written at the upper right above the date, or at the lower left below the body of the letter. Mrs. Hobart writes of her housekeeper, who is leaving to be near relatives in another town:

Louise Dahl has been in my service as housekeeper for six years. She is neat and efficient, and pleasant in the home, and is skilled at every-day cooking.

I should have been glad to retain Louise, but she prefers now to work in Eau Claire. The fact that she has been in one position six years is a recommendation in itself.

> J. T. Hobart
> (Mrs. John Hobart)

The Willows
309 River Avenue
Delevan, Wisconsin

One might read between the lines that Louise was no fancy, party cook, but this fact may or may not interest the prospective employer.

Mrs. Hobart writes a note to the milkman before a trip.

Mr. Mueller,
We shall be away for about a month, so please leave nothing until further notice. I shall notify the dairy when we return.

> Mrs. J. C. Hobart

Before arriving home after the trip, Mrs. Hobart drops a note to the new housekeeper to notify her of their coming.

Dear Olga,
Mr. Hobart, the children, and I expect to arrive Tuesday about six. Will you plan a dinner for 6:30? Get something that can be kept hot: roast, scalloped potatoes, new squash, salad, and pie for dessert.

Mr. Hobart asks me to say the thought of one of your cherry pies makes his mouth water now.

> J. T. Hobart

March 28

WELCOMING A NEW RECTOR

While she is away, Mrs. Hobart hears from home that her family's church has a new rector. She writes a letter of greeting to the rector's wife:

Mrs. Walter Milnes
Rectory of Saint Michael's Church
Delevan, Wisconsin

My dear Mrs. Milnes,

To be away from Delevan and not be able to join in welcoming you is one of the drawbacks of not being home this winter. There are certainly occasions when it would be helpful to be in two places at one time. However, I know I shall soon have the pleasure of meeting you. I feel sure you will enjoy Delevan. It is a very pretty town, and Saint Michael's parish is an active one.

My husband joins me in extending our best wishes to you and Dr. Milnes for a happy life with us at Saint Michael's.

> Most sincerely yours,
> Janet Hobart
> (Mrs. J. C. Hobart)

TO FAMILY AND INTIMATE FRIENDS

To a Daughter Away at School

April 2

Dearest Ruth,

This has been a busier week than usual after our six weeks away. You were sweet to have a letter here to greet me. Thank you, dear. My hasty note told you of our arrival. The house was in spic and span order and Olga, who likes to fuss more than Louise did, had baked a cherry pie in our honor. Fluff has had five new kittens, two tiger and three grey. There are crocuses up in the front lawn. Tulips, hyacinths, and jonquils will be on their way soon. We ought to have some spring gardens worth seeing when you arrive Easter Monday. I have a new chintz slip cover for your room with tulips in gay yellows and pinks. Peter is likely to be stuck in the mud with his bike. He got it out before he came in the house.

Last night we had Dr. and Mrs. Milnes and their four children dine with us. They are delightful people. Peter and Jim are already sworn pals. Judy is having a real problem in school. Mrs. Milnes was concerned that schools might be different here, and she was right. The girl is simply lost with no Latin and no French. She is a good student, and I began to wonder whether she wouldn't be able to settle her problems at Riverview. I talked immediately with Mrs. Milnes about the idea, and the upshot is that I phoned Dr. Kenyon to see about a scholarship. Judy will be with you tomorrow if all works out. Now, Ruth, will you be a committee to see that she doesn't get lonesome the first day? She will make friends right away, I know, and will give you girls some stiff competition in class. She has pretty brown hair and merry eyes, but I can see she has been worried and unhappy over her school work.

No more now, my dear. Your father will be driving to La Crosse for you in a couple of weeks if he can. Your friends that I have seen, Cora, Betty, Tom, Hazel, Bill, all send their regards. Roller skates are all over the sidewalks in town, and Pete is playing ball again.

> With love,
> Mother

Asking for Advice

Ruth writes from Riverview for advice.

Dear Dad,

I am in a great quandary. To take them or not to take them! That is the question. Put the college board exams for the object, and my uncertain future for the reason for my indecision and you get a fair picture of my mental attitude. If I go to the University of Wisconsin where I do not need a record in examinations, there is no reason to go through the strain and stress of writing them; and I shall be perfectly happy at Wisconsin and certainly have excellent courses from which to choose, especially should I take history, science, or journalism. The historical library is second only to Harvard's, I understand, and the lecturers the finest to be found, all of them truly scientific historians. There is no place where one has more fun along with work than at Madison. I'll have a grand time there, Dad.

Then, on the other hand, I seem headed for the classics and modern language! I can specialize in that, too, at the University. And yet why have I studied so hard to prepare for the exams if I side-step them at the end? Do you think there is any likelihood of my going to Westminster? I'm glad I've studied to learn all this stuff. What shall I do?

In most profound perplexity,
Ruth

April 4

Dear Ruth,

Your letter shows that you are giving serious thoughts to the arrangement of your future and that your type of training is bearing fruit. I can see that there really isn't any doubt in your mind about taking the examinations. That's as it should be, and there need be no worrying over writing an examination when you'll know the answers. It is rather an opportunity for seeing how well you can handle the tools that you have been learning to use.

I like to have you well grounded in the literature and philosophy of other centuries and of other countries than our own. You have thereby an excellent standard by which to judge what you meet that is new and modern. You have time while you are young to do the drill work. You can read Latin, French, and English literature with appreciation. You can branch into the field of history and geography. You will enjoy travel and can meet people of other lands with a sympathy for their background. That is one reason for my having entered you at Riverview. I believe that in our new world there will be great opportunities for young people without prejudice.

I shall be happy to have you study at Westminster and meet young women from other sections of our country. When you are a little older, I think you will be able to assimilate better the advantages of University work with the broadening influence of the masculine point of view.

Good luck to you in your examinations and may the readers of the papers feel as sure as I do of your ability to handle your material. Your Latin vocabulary is good. You speak French easily.

Your affectionate
Dad

April 7

From a Young Son at Camp

Camp Minnieska
Lac Court d'Oreilles
August 8

Dear Dad,

This camp is great. Yesterday I caught a muskelunge. Well, at least I brought it up to the boat. I felt a jerk on the line, reeled in, saw Mr. Muskie jump and then pull the line out spinning. I reeled him in again. Oh, he was a beauty! He jumped and jerked, and put up a lot of tricks. He made the reel fly so fast, it took a piece right out of my first finger. The last time I brought him to the boat, Mr. Hawkins shot him. Eighteen pounds he weighed, and we had muskie steak for supper with blueberry muffins.

The Indians know how to cook fish. They roll it in corn meal, Jake, our guide, says. I should like to have sent the fish home to you and Mother; but I have eaten so much of the others' fish, I was glad to have one to offer. I think, anyway, bass will suit the size of our range better, and they are good. I'll bring some.

But, Dad, may I stay another week? I'm learning a lot here. I think it would be good. Please let me.

Your loving son,
Peter

The Willow Farm
August 12

Dear Peter,

To have you like Court d'Oreilles is very good news to me, I have spent some of my best vacations fishing in those waters, and I can taste your muskie steaks in retrospect. This time, Peter, I think we must limit the outing to two weeks. You are needed here for some chores while the men are harvesting. Do not be too disappointed, for I have another surprise in store for you. How would you like to go north to Burntside with me at partridge season? After the farm is put in shape for the winter I can get away for a week, and I had planned to take you with me in October—provided, of course, your grades in school are averaging B+. You can compare the north woods of Minnesota with Wisconsin's timber lands.

We'll be expecting you in a few days, then. The new cider is tiptop this year. The apples were never better.

Your loving
Dad

Between School Friends

Burntside Lake
Ely, Minnesota
October 15

Dear Bob,

Burntside is a lake you must see some day. There are bears here. One came down a Norway trunk right by my window this morning. There are deer in the swamp a half mile back of the cabin. All the cabins up here built by the Finnish people are of Norway logs. No nails are used.

To get to the hunting: We have an Indian guide who has taken us across our arm of the lake and over a portage. There we have found partridge perched on the limbs of the trees, sitting on rocks or scurrying off the path. Partridge are stupid things. I've been in a car and seen a partridge sitting on a fence. There he sits while the driver stops the car, gets out, puts his gun together and shoots. In cold weather a partridge will conceal its head in a hole near the root of a tree, presumably to keep warm and let its exposed body freeze. Partridge are easily prepared. And are they good to eat! Partridge with corn and wild rice is a supper for a king. The Indians boil their birds and have stew, but we wrapped each one with a couple of strips of bacon and cooked them in a large iron skillet.

You and your dad will have to plan to come here next open season.

Your pal,
Peter

When Peter was camping at Burntside Lake, the little dog that had been loaned him for company got into difficulties with a porcupine. Peter had to take him into town to the veterinarian, but as he found no one at the office, he had to leave a note:

Friday afternoon

Dear Dr. Thompson,

Will you call me at the Parkman residence, 182 J, as soon as you return? My dog, Bob, has quills in his muzzle that I can't extract. When I heard the commotion behind the cabin, I found the "porkie" with his nose between the logs. Bob was dancing around him, barking. I lured Bob in the cabin with a piece of meat and started taking out the quills. All around his mouth they were thick. Then he opened his mouth and several had lodged in his throat and the roof of his mouth. He was very quiet while I took out those. The ones in his nose have hooked themselves in. He needs your attention as soon as you can take care of him.

Hastily yours,
Peter Hobart

When Ruth was spending a few days camping on the Red Cedar River with a schoolmate from Menomonie, she wrote a note to her mother to share some of her good times with the family:

Menomonie, Wisconsin
August 15

Dear Mother,

I'm having such a good time camping with Eff and her friends at "Buzzard's Roost" on the point! Naturally, we practically live in bathing suits. We swim, we follow this winding river upstream and downstream, across little lakes made by the dams put in by the old lumber company or the new electric power company. One dam was constructed just last year, so the water has only recently risen to any height. We were paddling our canoes yesterday among the tops of trees and could reach out and bring branches with birds' nests right up to us. It seemed like a fairy land setting on a stage. We dive out the end of a row boat, swim awhile, then climb back in. We dry out while eating luncheon in some pretty spot.

Every evening we have a bonfire and sing songs. The girls' boy friends from town usually drop in to see us when the "Uncle Sam" makes its evening trip. That is the pokey old excursion boat that churns up and down the river every night, twice on Sundays, and other times by appointment for a dozen passengers. It will accommodate thirty or forty easily. We brought all our camp supplies on it. The water is deep enough at our dock for it to pull alongside.

Last night Eff's parents had come to pay us a visit and to bring more baked beans. After the boat was part way to town, we all thought it would be fun to row in for ice cream. Eff and I were at the oars. We took the row boat so as to take all five. We began to gain on "Uncle Sam." As we came nearer, we saw all the passengers watching our race. We drew up about even as we left the river channel and started to cross the little lake at the town. Eff's father called to us that he'd treat us all if we reached the pier before the boat. Eff is on the crew at Milwaukee Downer, so she was in practice for distance rowing. We hoped our strength would equal our enthusiasm. You understand "Uncle Sam" can go only so fast—which speed isn't great, but it can keep it up.

On we went, one of the girls at the rudder counting strokes for us and the other two singing to keep time for our rhythm. We really felt ourselves pulling away. The people on "Uncle Sam" sent up a shout as we outdistanced them. Then we tied up at the pier and helped Mr. and Mrs. Berwick step off their boat as it wheezed a last wheeze. Did that ice cream taste good! I'm sure a race on the Thames or Hudson could mean no more to the rowers than our race did to us.

Thanks so much for the food you sent. It arrived safely and quickly disappeared.

> Much love to you, Dad, and Peter,
> Ruth

> Saint Mary's Hall
> Shrub Oak, N. Y.
> November 1

Dear Ruth,

Sally writes me that you are in the hospital. It's hard to believe; you've always been so healthy. Well, the appendix is just an old left-over of when we were gorillas, or something, so you're well rid of it!

The Army-Columbia game was great. I guess you may have read that it ended 27-26 in Army's favor, and it was close all the way. The band and cheerleaders were marvelous, and the boys look so smart in their uniforms. I would have enjoyed going with Grant more if I hadn't met Phyllis' brother, Jack, last Easter. He's been writing me since I visited there, and he hopes to get up to school to see me some weekend soon.

I'm sending you a funny book. At least, I hope *you'll* think it's funny.

I hope you will be entirely recovered for Christmas vacation. Oh, you will be—in six weeks you will have forgotten you ever had an appendix. I'll help you with Aeneas and try to speak French if you have to make up lessons.

Affectionately,
Helene

Riverview School
La Crosse, Wisconsin
December 5

Dear Helene,

Thanks so much for the book. After I'd laughed myself silly over it I showed it to the nurses, and they passed it all around among them. The good laughs and the special treatment the nurses have given me since speeded my recovery.

No sooner was I back at school than I was deep in plans for the Christmas party. There is a tea given in the afternoon for the parents and guests who arrive early, a dinner just for the students, the chapel service for everyone, a short play, usually of a religious nature, and then the dance. One class has charge of the tea, one of the play, and the other of the dance, so no one is too rushed.

If the weather is good, Mother and Dad will drive up for me. But if the prediction is storms for Friday and Saturday, I will go home by train.

I shall be so anxious to see you and to hear about your festivities and your friend, Jack. The last three days I was in the hospital, Miss Swift came up an hour each day and translated my Latin lessons to me. It was surprising how much I remembered when it came to our tests. Miss Miller took me the first Monday after my return and told me in French the story of what I'd missed, so there was just English and Math to do, and that seemed to fit in all right. We have no lessons to do in vacation, but I plan to review some. Those college boards do loom bigger and bigger on the horizon.

Much love,
Ruth

29 Oak Terrace
Delevan, Wisconsin
April 15

Dear Mrs. McConnell,

Your daughter Julie told me when I called that you are off on vacation, and I rather hesitate to write this to you, except that the happiness of our Girl Scouts depends on it. Mrs. Dann, my co-leader, and I have promised them a campout the weekend of May 16. This begins Friday afternoon, includes Saturday and Sunday until after lunch. We have canvassed most of the mothers in the troop to help chaperon, but they all have younger children whom they are reluctant to leave for so long.

Your Ellen told us you might be able to come with us as Julie is so self-sufficient. She also said your family has gone on several camping trips. (You can probably teach me a few tricks!) We should have at least four chaperones for our troop. Mrs. Reichard is coming, and you'd be an ideal fourth!

Ellen would be thrilled to have her mother come, and the rest of us would be so grateful.

Think it over and phone me when you return home.

Yours cordially,
Wilma Hauck

Requesting Information

If one wants an immediate reply to some request, he will write a rather brief letter containing merely the request and a pleasant greeting.

Hillside School
Brewster, N. Y.
March 27

Dear Aunt Tat,

Will you help a fellow out of difficulties? I've been appointed chairman of the decorations for a matinee dance in May. We've had a boat, a Dutch garden, a ski train, a Chinese tea house, Tahiti, and goodness knows what else. You've never let me down before. Do come forward with something handsome and practical.

Mother writes that everything at our house is going on as usual. I hope you and Uncle Bob will be going over in two weeks when I have Saturday and Sunday at home.

Your loving nephew,
Dale

The reply will also be limited to the answering of the question. The writer thus shows he has given his mind wholly to the request.

Birthday Letter

A letter from a devoted family member adds to the joys of the birthday boy or girl, young or old:

July 17

Dear Jeanie,

It's hard to believe that some twelve years ago you were a tiny pink bundle lying in a bassinet under the mantel here. You were the prettiest baby! All you wanted was a little food and lots of attention. When you cried your Daddy held you in the palm of his hand or slung you over his shoulder, and you were comforted.

And now—look at you—a big, lovely bundle full of pep and bursting with vitality, ready to improve the world with clever ideas and winning ways.

Grow bigger and better in charm and graciousness with each added year, so that we'll be prouder and prouder of you on the new birthdays. I wish I could be with you to help celebrate, but I'll be thinking of you and wishing you the best of everything.

Affectionately,
Your Grandma

Graduation Letter

12 Robin Crescent
Chandler, Illinois
June 10

Dear Harold,

It seems such a short time ago that I was visiting your mother, and we watched you skipping off to kindergarten in a blue suit, size

6. And now you are finished with the exciting and demanding years of college, ready to start on a fine career. They tell me engineers are in demand today, and believe me, any organization that gets you will be most fortunate.

While some people are always wringing their hands at the state of the world, it is the entrance into that world of fine, conscientious young people like yourself that keeps my hopes high.

With my congratulations and love,
Devotedly,
Aunt Marian

Requesting Money

Riverview School
La Crosse, Wisconsin
December 10

Dear Mother,

This seems to be the season for gifts again. We have one for the head of the school, for our class advisor, for the chaplain, for all the maids, for the janitor, for the offering in the chapel, and then there are ones for the girls here in school. I've seen a few accessories I rather need for my dress for the dance, and as you may have guessed, I have only two dollars left from my allowance.

How am I to plan for all these expenses? Is it a good thing to borrow on my future allowance, can I look for a bonus at Christmas because of good marks in exams, or do I just out and out ask for help? Can you send some sort of relief to your impoverished

Barbara

SCHOOL MATTERS

RIVERVIEW SCHOOL
LA CROSSE, WISCONSIN

January 15

Dearest Mother,

Miss Lawrence will write you about my work, I'm sure. I hope it won't be too much of a shock to you, but I don't make any progress and there isn't any use spending Dad's money to keep me here. I can't keep track of Caesar's daily marches. There is another pet pastime they have here, and that's finding what x equals. I try, but I just can't care at all; it can equal any old thing it wants to. I generally try to accommodate and put down something, but it's usually wrong.

Then all the fun the girls enjoy is chasing a ball of some kind around, and what the sense is in putting a ball inside a hoop, or over a net, or between posts, I don't see.

Miss Lawrence was most understanding. She knows I like to care for little children, and she told me about a school where I can take courses about care of children, cooking, sociology, go on with biology, take applied arithmetic, and story telling. I'm a flop at this, but I'm sure I shouldn't be at that. I could start second semester if you'll let me. When I get through I could work in nursery school or care for small children. Maybe I'd learn how to keep house. I'd like very much to try. Do you want me to take the exams? I got 26 on my last algebra test.

Oh, Mother, this is awful. Do save me!

> Devotedly,
> Anne

January 15

Darling,

Your letter and one from Miss Lawrence came in the same mail. You seem to have had a very practical talk together, arriving at the conclusion that a course in home economics and one in arts and crafts would be beneficial for you. Daddy and I drove over to Red Wing last evening to see the school Miss Lawrence mentioned and to interview Miss Taylor. In the art room we saw the weaving that girls had been doing and stencils for decoration on a nursery wall. The kitchen is a busy place during class hours. One class had served a luncheon for eight guests yesterday. There is a lovely sunny nursery and a small playground for the children who come during the day. Miss Taylor says she has placed several girls as day nursery assistants.

We liked the girls we met, and expect that you will, too.

You ask about your examinations. Yes, take them, by all means. You always want to finish what you start just as well as you can. If you had 26 on your last algebra test, perhaps you can make 36 this time. Try your best—you might surprise yourself, you know.

> Lovingly,
> Mother

61 Mill Lane
Delevan, Wisconsin
March 14

Mrs. John Cummings
Librarian, Delevan High School
City

My dear Mrs. Cummings,

Our dramatic society has decided to use the proceeds from the junior play this year to buy books for the library. We should like to make a suggestion about purchases—subject, of course, to your approval. As we all study English history the second semester of our junior year, don't you think it advisable to increase the number of reference books in that section of the library?

We shall leave the selection of specific books to you since you have access to all the bookseller's lists and know reading of lasting value. We should like also to add to the record collection. Here may we suggest a selection of modern composers, including some Americans? Could you allocate half the sum for books and half for records, approximately?

We hope that you and the whole school will find pleasure in our gift.

Most sincerely yours,
Cora Strong
Secretary of the Dramatic Society

MEN IN SERVICE

Men in military service like to hear all the gossip of the home town. They want to feel they are remembered as part of the activities they left.

Mrs. Hobart's nephew writes her from overseas:

APO 326
c/o Postmaster
New York City
December 8

Dear Aunt Janet,

It was good to get your letter all about the family and Delevan. I hope Ruth recovered from her operation all right. You and Uncle

John are certainly enjoying your grandson. Little Mike will be able to talk when I get back, I guess.

Our C.O. is a good sort and Uncle Sam feeds us well. The food does not taste like home, but there is plenty of it. We have movies, a TV in the rec hall, and plenty of games there. There's one fellow here from La Crosse and another from a farm near the lake. I've made several good friends, and we've gone into the town on a few nights off. The young people are friendly. Many speak English. The older people hang back, though. The girls are pretty, but the only kind of clothes most of them can get are sleazy.

Most of the stores here are little shops, where there's no hurry, and the buildings are either centuries old or ultra-modern. I'm collecting many souvenirs, especially for Peter.

We have a great basketball team. I sub on it now. We just trounced the civilian workers' team last week. From duty, athletics, drilling, etc., I've lost five pounds.

Say "Hello" to all the Delevan fellows. Maybe I'll be seeing Gene over here from what he writes. Thank you for your letter. Write again soon. Merry Christmas and Happy New Year to you all.

Sincerely,
Bart

Delevan, Wisconsin
January 27

Dear Bart,

Your aunt showed me the letter you wrote before Christmas. You must be seeing the world, which is a real opportunity. I hope I'll be that lucky.

The town is on its toes in basketball. Our squad has won from Elkhart, Janeston, Whiteriver, and Sugar Creek. There's Richearth still and two return games; but if we ever had a look-in at the championship, it's right now. At the Whiteriver spring tournament the end of next month, we ought to show up pretty well. Paul Grant and Olaf Helgesen are the stars. Olaf holds top honors in points scored in the Southeastern Six so far. The townspeople are turning out in crowds for every game.

We're having rather warm weather for this season. The lake is thawing already. The men are coming in from their fishing huts. At night, the sound of the ice cracks widening is weird at this time of year. Naturally no skiing, no skating. But then, we go to the Armory for roller skating. You would enjoy some of the couples that are pairing off this winter—Bill has followed Hannah persistently for six weeks, Ardiss has finally corralled Bob, and the Bascom twins have definitely settled down to the inseparables, Gretchen and Patty.

Do you remember Doris Crane who was a year ahead of you and sang the lead in the senior musical? Well, just as everyone predicted, she got ahead! She just won a contract singing on TV. She was back in town last week. You'd hardly know her. She's a redhead now.

Some builder has bought the Olesen farm and is putting up rows of very neat houses. Hurry home before the place changes too much. We all miss you and your sax.

As ever,
Don

TO FRIENDS WHO HAVE MOVED AWAY

One of the best services of letters is to sustain a friendship between good neighbors and friends who have moved away or live at a distance.

October 10

Dear Faith,

By now you must be well settled in Elmhurst and, being you, you must have made many friends already. I hope Jim likes his work at Consolidated. I'm sure they like *him!*

It seems unnatural not to have you right next door. We miss you all, and I miss our morning coffees. Michael keeps looking for Bob. He can't understand where he's gone. And I miss Bob's looking out for Michael.

The Bradburys, who moved in to your house seem very nice. Her baby is only two months old and her little boy eighteen months, so she has little time to visit. They like your house, she said, and love the garden. Mr. B. does the gardening, and he's always pruning and weeding.

The Fowlers down at 27 just got a beagle. But the beagle, named Jinx, has adopted us and sleeps on our steps. I suspect Michael has given it some bones from the trash can and also some fresh ground beef, of which I keep missing small handfuls. Scotty is quite jealous, naturally.

John and I plan to visit his parents in Quebec at Christmas. I'm brushing up on my French at adult school just to surprise them. Little

Michael is a delight, although a strenuous one. He had a temper tantrum last week and was so cute that John and I both laughed. We'll never do that again. He was so really offended.

All of us send our best to the best of neighbors. You must come back here next summer. Write me all your news and all about life in Elmhurst.

                              Love,
                                   Joan

CHRISTMAS NOTES

The good will of the Christmas season brings forth Christmas notes on cards and holiday note paper. A note should be kept brief at this busy season; it should be full of holiday wishes and news of special interest to the recipient. Some families have a Christmas letter mimeographed with all the family news, which, while it keeps friends posted, is quite impersonal without handwritten additions.

Christmas cards or notes are addressed to *Mr. and Mrs.* even if "Mrs." is not known to the family. They are signed *Joan and John Lacerte,* not *Mr. and Mrs. John Lacerte,* although a family card can be signed *The John Lacertes.*

                                              December 18
Dear Dot and Dick,

Here's wishing you all a Merry Christmas and a New Year bright with joy and success. How is your darling Patricia? Michael now talks incessantly although not always coherently. He's ready to burst waiting for Santa. One of our New Year's plans is to have you visit us. I'll write soon.

                              Love,
                                   Joan

If we all resolve to keep up correspondence with our friends through the year, our Christmas notes can then be brief and cheerful like Joan's.

INDEX